The Dynamics

of

Living Love

*To
Carol
Best Wishes
Charlie Summers*

THE DYNAMICS

OF

LIVING LOVE

Charles Sommer

DeVorss *Publications*

ISBN: 0-87516-668-7

Library of Congress Catalog Card Number: 93-74407

DeVorss & Company, *Publisher*
Box 550
Marina del Rey, CA 90294

Printed in the United States of America

Contents

PART III

PART IV

An Acknowledgment

Almighty, omnipotent God, of myself I can do nothing. There is no greater joy than finding myself in Thee; we Love Pilgrims are at Thy command, our eternal Shepherd, glowing and growing as Love would have us be.

Fear only seems to separate us. It is through the immaculate concept, the living Christ, that You conceived us out of Yourself. O Father God, out of Your Goodness, You provide the Holy Comforter, the Divine Mother, the Wayshower. You impel us, compel us, to express Love, for that is what we are. Even when we falter, You are there. The Aquarian dispensation in this new age brings forth a deeply moral super-humanity ennobled by the universal spirit of the cosmic Christ. Through the arts, sciences and religions, a new global humanity emerges, as each Love Pilgrim answers the clarion call to selfless service.

This book is dedicated to the Love Pilgrims who have no bottom line . . . Love Pilgrims are at the center of everything and at the border of no thing. Love Pilgrims are the pioneers of the twenty-first century. We are found everywhere Love is expressed.

I am most grateful to a caring mother, and to a most

understanding wife and family, who each in their own way have taught me Love; thank you. To my three sons and their wives, my extended family and relatives, who each in their own way have taught me Love, thank you. To Henry Drummond and all the contributors to this book, thank you very much. Also, I would like to express my gratitude for editorial assistance from Dorothy Boyer, Emily Kay Michael, Carol Karpeck, and my spouse, author and friend Bobbe L. Sommer, Ph.D. Those who found and are finding the courage to live their soul purpose, I am dedicating this book to you. I am also dedicating this book to my mother, Lucy J. Sommer, who went the distance for all her children. She is known to many that have adopted her as Mom, Grandma, Great-Grandma, or just Aunt Lu. I love and bless you.

PRELUDE

THE question is, "What is Love?" A simple answer and profound idea is, "God is Love." If that is true, as we express Love we are God-like. To know God is to know God in Spirit. That Spirit is Love.

There is no greater need in these troubled times than to express Love for the good health of ourselves, our families, our neighbors and the global community. Within the Spirit of Love, all the good solutions come to the surface. Love always provides a workable answer.

Love is the mysterious power that generates wholesome, creative, beneficial activity. President Clinton said in his inaugural address, "There is nothing wrong that can't be cured by what is right." Love is right. It is the fulfillment of *Divine Law*. The Law responds to us in kind. Our choices in life, reduced down to the lowest common denominator are: either teaching fear or expressing Love.

The mother who would like to hear more frequently from her married son gets angry with him. When he finally calls, she uses fault and blame as her weapons. This is not Love speaking; it is fear . . . the fear within the mother that prevents her from contacting that son to inform him that she misses and loves him. It is often the fear of rejection that causes us to project our fears onto others as blame and shame. We think we will be rejected, and *we* do the rejecting first by finding fault. We thereby cast a shadow instead of a light.

This book is written for Love Pilgrims who are interested in fine-tuning relationships, living life more dynamically and creatively. Many examples of what dynamically works and what does not work are provided. The dynamics of Love are explained and encouraged.

The basic theory is that Love is an art and the form it takes is up to us. Love as Law responds in kind. Love as a gift is the God-like remedy that works. No one has all the answers to life's vast array of challenges; yet each of us does have access to Love, which provides the answers from an infinite Source of intelligence.

Professor Henry Drummond's 100-year-old work called *The Greatest Thing in the World* is used as a stepping-stone for the ideas developed and presented here. Drummond's work was built on his understanding of science, religion, and philosophy. He proved to his students that "The supreme gift to covet is Love."

Living Love is the most dynamic choice we can make. To be good at expressing Love requires practice and meta-cognitive awareness. In plain words, understanding the dynamics, having the desire and producing focused effort will transform the student by renewing their mind to their God-like nature.

CONGRATULATIONS! You have become more interested in Love and have attracted this book unto yourself through the Law of Attraction. There is nothing new about Love. Much has been written, spoken and expressed. In order for us to synthesize Love, we must understand Love. We must feel Love. We must express Love. Love is our essential nature, and we are all linked together in Spirit. Each of us is a vital link. We are on an evolutionary journey awakening to Love.

We must express Love to realize it. We don't make it real. It *is* real. It *is* the answer that brings the best possible results. Something in us knows that expressing true Love is the most intelligent choice we can make.

No religion, philosophy, political or national persuasion, has a monopoly on Love. Every person, every race, every ism, technology, institution, can benefit by exploring the depth and breadth of Love—a primordial power that we know little about. This thing called Love is the Life force. We are imbued with this Life force, yet we know very little about Love, which expresses through Law.

Love/Law

The concept of Law is simple. What we sow is what we reap. We plant a watermelon seed and we get a watermelon. What do seeds called Love look like? How do we recognize Love? How can we expand Love in our lives? This is a more complex subject. We understand Love is a quality recognized in deity, in God. We know Love is also an attribute of humankind. Love is a power like electricity. If we understand it, we can use it more effectively. If we are ignorant of the Law through which Love is expressed, we can get burned. For where there is Love there is Law. Love transforms and transcends human suffering. It is the greatest power.

This author intends to give many personal examples of what Love is, how to recognize it and how to expand it. We all have some misguided or inept ideas on the subject, and I hope this book may assist you in clarifying and expanding your ideas and concepts.

Love Often Requires Effort

God knows we all can be lazy and stubborn. It can require commitment and effort to open one's mind, to seek Truth. As this book developed, I realized that Love really is the greatest thing in the world. Love is always there, its spark waiting to be ignited by us. Many of us wait for Love to come to us. The magic is that it can only come *through* us. We must take an active part in bringing it through us to realize its greatness. That requires work.

Love Requires Remodeling

Did you ever remodel a house? We may start with one room, or one idea, and we know we can't stop there till there is full restoration. That is the truth about Love. That is the truth about renewing our minds. There may be a concept, or belief, we hold about Love that is limiting our growth. If there is something in the text of this book that stirs your mind and opens your heart, it is because you are ready to change.

Gratitude

I am so grateful to the many people of all ages who have helped me realize Love. The little children, the young couples, the adolescents, the singles set, the teenagers, the parents, the matured adults. All, in their own way, have made a contribution to this book. All, in their own way have made a statement about Love.

A wonderful old book that was a gift to my wife ended up on my own personal bookshelves. I needed more space for new books. While I was cleaning out some old books, I found this small gem by Professor Henry Drummond. I was very reluctant to write about the gift of Love before I found his works. Over a hundred years ago this Scottish professor, with his simplicity, clarity and style, reached many college students through his lectures. Some of Professor Drummond's lectures and addresses were published and became an instantaneous success.

I am using his works as the foundation of this book. These works are used as a springboard into the many benefits of developing and using the gift of Love. Drummond's writings contrasted, analyzed and defended Love as THE GREATEST THING IN THE WORLD. I am most impressed with his works. I went to the Scottish

National Library in Edinburgh, Scotland, and read all that I could find by him and about him.

Doing research for this book has been very enjoyable. I've discovered most of the teachers of Love that I respect were unique. Jesus the Christ, Saint Paul, Saint John, Joan of Arc, Saint Francis of Assisi, Mother Teresa are all Christians and all expressed Love differently. Jiddu Krishnamurti, Ralph Waldo Emerson, Leo Buscaglia, Gerry Jampolski, Mahatma Gandhi, Martin Luther King—their lives express Love in ways unique to them. Ernest Holmes, Albert Einstein, Abraham Maslow, M. Scott Peck and many more had arrived at a notion similar to Professor Drummond's. Drummond said, "There is nothing more needed in this generation than a larger and more scriptural idea of God."

The *idea* that has been manifested by the deepest spiritual intuition of every generation is this: There is a Divine Presence and a Spiritual Law that are expressed as Love. Different religions call it by various names, such as Christ, Buddha, Atman, Avatar, Anointed, Messiah or Enlightened One.

Our relationship with:

1. God, Spirit, or the whole of Life, Nature
2. Each other
3. Self

is best realized by us as we express love. Love is fulfilling the Law of Being through us. What does that mean? God's will for us is to express Love. Love is individualized through us.

Love is God's Law being fulfilled. By right use of the Law we succeed . . . we become more Christlike. *Willfulness* is a deterrent, it is self-centeredness. *Willingness* to reform and conform to God's will is the key. God-centeredness is Love. Love God, Love one's self, Love each other. The Law is simple, but do we really understand how it works?

Ask yourself, is planet earth a finishing school? Does life end with death? Or are we in a reformatory school here on this planet? Is there an omnipresent, all-powerful God punishing us or teaching us? If we are here to learn something, what would it be? If heaven and earth pass away, of what value are they if we did not learn to love?

If God's will for us is Love, then fearing God is not the answer. It has been my experience and observation that ''perfect Love casts out fear.'' There is something at the core of us that knows this is true. For us to express Love—desire, interest, understanding and discipline are vital and necessary.

My intention is to offer some ideas and personal examples of how Love works through Law. Love works through Spiritual Law. Understanding is the foundation of Intelligence and Love is the foundation of understanding. The way to get Love, is to give it.

I trust the material presented in this book will shed some light on the subject. My Love for God and my Love for you have prompted me to share this with you. Do I have all the answers? No. What I have endeavored to do was to assimilate ancient principles into current-day understanding. Believing in Love is not the same as living it. False beliefs lead us astray or blind us from the real expression of Love.

Analytical People

If you are a very analytical person you may appreciate the scientific approach used by Drummond and me. A true scientist is also a mystic, willing to venture more deeply into the parts of life to discover the whole—the mystical adventure to make the unknown knowable, to discern the esoteric in the exoteric. Discovering the dynamic laws of love and how they work is very important to our wellbeing. If you are more like the social scientist, the simple yet vivid examples of real people in current settings will reach you where you live.

A word of caution and a touch of humor someone recently shared with me, I now share with you. ''Don't let your dogma get run over by your karma.'' That is good advice. As you read and reread this material, suspend your judgments (dogma) and feel the underlying basis for understanding the meaning of Love. It is no accident that you have ventured thus far. If your belief system gets validated or provoked into a greater appreciation for the ''Dynamic of Living Love,'' so be it.

Professor Henry Drummond

Let me now share with you Henry Drummond. As a professor of science and as an ordained minister in the Free

Church of Scotland, he was loved. His teaching was "never allusive, superior, strained; he does not condescend. He is always himself, a courteous, unaffected gentleman, with a sincere respect for his audience." Drummond thought that the greatest thing in the world is Love.

Drummond believed that we need a greater appreciation for the Allness of God. "I discovered myself enunciating spiritual Law in the exact terms of Biology and Physics. We have Truth in Nature as it comes from God. And it has to be read with the same unbiased mind, the same reverence as all other Revelations," says Drummond. "Love is not a thing of emotion and gush. It is a robust, strong, vigorous expression of the whole character and nature in its fullest development. And these things are only acquired by daily and hourly practice," he said.

"Life is full of opportunities for learning Love. Every man and woman every day has a thousand of them. The world is not a playground; it is a school room. The greatest lesson that we are always to learn is the lesson of Love in all its parts."

"If the purification of religion comes from science, the purification of science comes from religion," according to Drummond.

Drummond uses St. Paul's thoughts on Love as the foundation for his lectures. St. Paul is a good choice. Paul was no stranger to conflict and disharmony both before and after his illuminating experience on the road to Damascus. Paul was ruled by his great intellect and his passion for law. This man of Tarsus knew the laws of the Jews and the Gentiles well. Paul instigated and watched the death of Stephen, the first person to die for this new faith that taught Love. Paul's passion for law and order lacked compassion. But through the grace of God, his hardened heart awakened to Love. His mind now renewed itself. He took his new awareness and became an undaunted teacher of what he understood that God wants.

Paul now understood that Love is the will of God. That Love is the fulfillment of God's Law. And that each of us can discover that the greatest thing in the world is Love.

Though I speak with the tongues of men and of angels, and have not Love, I am become as sounding brass, or a tinkling cymbal. And though I have the gift of prophecy, and understand all mysteries, and all knowledge; and though I have all faith, so I could remove mountains, and have not Love, I am nothing. And though I bestow all my goods to feed the poor, and though I give my body to be burned, and have not Love, it profiteth me nothing.

Love suffereth long, and is kind;
Love envieth not;
Love vaunteth not itself, is not puffed up,
Doth not behave itself unseemly,
Seeketh not her own,
Is not easily provoked,
Thinketh no evil;
Rejoiceth not in iniquity,
but rejoiceth in the truth;
Beareth all things, believeth all things,
hopeth all things,
endureth all things.

Love never faileth: but whether there be prophecies, they shall fail; whether there be tongues, they shall cease; whether there be knowledge, it shall vanish away. For now we know in part, and we prophesy in part. But when that which is perfect is come, then that which is in part shall be done away. When I was a child, I spake as a child, I understood as a child, I thought as a child: but when I became a man, I put away childish things. For now we see through a glass, darkly; but then face to face: now I know in part; but then shall I know even as also I am known. And now abideth faith, hope, Love, these three; but the greatest of these is Love.

1st Corinthians 13

PART I

LOVE: HOW TO RECOGNIZE IT

SOMETIMES we think we are loving and we are not. Sometimes we consider ourselves lovers and we are not. Sometimes others consider us loveless and we are not. It is important to be able to recognize Love. For we are all Pilgrims journeying to the Shrine of Love, and the Shrine is within ourselves. I hope you will enjoy the journey through this book; may it bring you closer to *your* inner shrine.

The spectrum of Love is vast, unlimited, undefinable, yet recognizable. Each teacher of Love gives clues and insights that lead us to a set of principles. The principles are useful guides to determine if we are indeed expressing Love.

If our intention is to be expressing more Love, it behooves us to recognize what Love *is* and *is not* according to St. Paul's understanding. We don't have to agree or disagree with Paul. We each have our own faculty of discernment, which leads to our own individual understanding. Each of us can develop the use of our "infundibulum," which is a physiological funnel used to invite a supra consciousness. The process of developing a supra consciousness, a dynamic lifestyle motivated by God, through infinite Love, is available to us now. Love does not happen *to* us; it happens *through* us. It is most valuable for us to understand the dynamics of living Love. The spectrum of Love has many ingredients or virtues that are included in the supreme principle, Love. They are:

Patience—bears, endures and suffers all things
Kindness
Generosity
Humility
Courtesy
Unselfishness
Good temper
Rejoices in truth—sincerity
Never fails
Hopes all things

What Love does not do:

Seek her own—vaunt, or puff up, oneself
Behave unseemly—fearful
Think evil
Rejoice in iniquity
Become easily provoked

Now that we have become acquainted with St. Paul's do's and doesn'ts of Love, what is next? Let us examine these do's and doesn'ts in terms of our relationships.

You will find from here forward many personal examples of what Love is and what it is not. At the end of each personal example, I place the virtue or virtues of Love in parentheses. You may come up with more qualities than I have noted. This is *not* a test. We are simply endeavoring to observe these qualities in ourself and others.

Sex and the Private Parts

Where does begetting start? Is there a Father/Mother God that started all this begetting? I like to study history, but I'll leave the genealogy of begetting to someone else. Until we moved into this information age, sex was very private. Now it is publicly brought into the home by cable television and into the movie theater. The mystery of sex is gone, but the force that brings two persons together remains a mystery. There is only one power, and that power is God. How we use that power is a choice God leaves up to our own free will. The enlightened choice is Love.

Many authors, like myself, shy away from writing about sex. "Shy" is another way of allowing fear to run us. Sex can be controversial, or so private, we don't discuss it. For example, when I was a young boy my mother would give me a note to hand to the pharmacist. The pharmacist, in return, would give me a brown paper-wrapped package. Unknown to me it contained sanitary napkins. Today, living in the information age, many of the old superstitions and taboos have disappeared. Where Truth sheds light, there is no shame, for God has made everything out of Love and Law—and we no longer consider menstrual periods to be taboo, or unclean, or to be kept secret.

(Love is kind to ourselves and each other)

The Sex Urge

The sex urge is appropriate or we would not have it. It is Mother Nature's way of saying "let's produce." However, it is not just for the production of offspring. It is the creative urge. How we interpret this urge or spend this energy is up to us. Where our interest is placed, the energy is spent. I'll come back to this later.

When I was a twelve-year-old boy, I played on a neighborhood baseball team. One evening, an eighteen-year-old on our team took me behind the bushes and made sexual advances. He was trying to convince me that what he was requesting of me was normal and that many of the older boys were doing it with him. I liked these new feelings of sexual arousal, but what he was requesting of me did not seem right.

(Love does not behave unseemly)

When I told the priest in the confessional about my sexual encounter, he hollered very loudly about my inappropriate use of "private parts." I felt completely embarrassed. After that experience, I made it a rule that I would only say my confession to the deaf monsignor. The priest's upset was like that of an angry parent. When we as parents get frightened, we want to yell or beat some sense into our kids. That is not Love. It is fear. It is our ego wanting to control others. Love is not about finding fault with the homosexual or with the scolding priest. Love is not a guilt trip on ourselves or others.

(Love behaves not unseemly)

Within Love is all the intelligence we require to make appropriate choices. Love may not seem reasonable to the egotistically-driven mind. Chances are, if we are motivated and driven by fear, we have lost sight of Love and therefore we may not be able to reason through our heart.

(Love is not easily provoked)

We can always reason with ourself. Ask ourself: "Is this choice I am making based on fear or Love?" God is right where we are, so the correct answer is always within us. Love is not about seeking pleasure and avoiding pain. Love is about Truth.

(Love rejoices in Truth)

How to Choose

As a married adult, I was embarrassed to purchase condoms. I would ask my wife to buy them for us. I had been taught that birth control was sinful. Finally, after three kids and twelve years of marriage, I was told by a priest in the confessional that it is a matter of conscience as to how I practiced birth control. I don't think the priest had the Pope's permission to give me that advice, so he must have been using his *infundibulum*. (This word will be explained later). His idea about birth control must have been inspired, because it paralleled my own thoughts and the thoughts of many other Catholics. Our baby doctor encouraged us to stop having kids, and I felt that each of us has the right to make our own choices—whether others agree or not. I don't have the answers for you and you don't have them for me. The ultimate authority is God. And where is God? God is within us. We are here to minister what God wants.

(Love rejoices in Truth)

Is Sex Love?

Is sex the same as Love? The obvious answer is both yes and no. Most of us would agree that acts of molestation, harassment, and rape don't qualify as acts of Love. Homosexual or bisexual acts may be loving or less than loving, depending on where they are coming from. For instance, lust is an inordinate desire. It is a craving that has not been processed through Love's faculty. Often it is an addiction to seeking pleasures, for finding happiness outside of ourselves. True happiness is in giving from our heart center.

Within Love is the creative urge. Sexual intercourse

is the vehicle which is designed to create an offspring. For Spirit to create the form of a child through us requires our cooperation. For Spirit to manifest Love in any form requires our cooperation.

(Love does not behave unseemly, or seek her own)

Celibacy and Abstinence

Celibacy, or sexual abstinence, may be an inspired choice or an unenlightened choice. No one can make that particular choice for us. Something within us knows if we are denying or accepting what God wants for us. God is always right where we are. It could not be any different. The sex urge, in the larger sense, is the spirit of creativity. There is only one Spirit, and we know It differentiates Itself in boundless ways. A true celibate has answered the creative urge within by expressing his/her creativity in nonsexual ways. Whatever we consider our calling to be is right for us.

(Love is sincere)

Sex in Sales

Many years ago, my chosen field was sales. One time, in a sales meeting, I shared with my peer group my feelings about sex in sales and how I felt the same creative energy that went into a sale also went into the act of sexual intercourse. Much to my surprise, the others laughed.

Yet something in me knew. If we love what we are doing, the creative juices flow. I have never met a person who was being creative, and fulfilling a desire to serve in a beneficial way, in a state of depression. Have you? Depression comes when we deny expression . . . the expression of Love.

(Giving, sharing our talents, is an act of kindness)

Recreational Sex

As my dear mentor Henry Drummond stated, we would not need rules like the Ten Commandments if we were coming from our heart center. True Love knows what is appropriate always. If we have any doubts as to where we are coming from, we'd best follow the Golden Rule. In so-called romantic Love, we create the interest that brings us together. If it is purely physical attraction or sexual addiction, it is doomed from the start. If there is a sincere caring, a bonding that goes beyond the need for sex, there is hope for the relationship.

(Love is sincere)

God does not deny us either pleasure or pain. Simply put, there is no escape from the consequences of our actions, whether those consequences be pleasurable or painful. The law of karma, cause and effect, compensation, is a two-edged sword. Unenlightened choices bring corresponding less-than-delightful results. Our soul carries within it the transcripts of where and how we have been.

What we do now is most important in shaping our future. Love is the greatest choice and the most beautiful expression—and will result in the most beneficial consequences for us.

I know a lady who contracted the AIDS virus more than ten years ago from a blood transfusion. She was having brain surgery for cancer and received infected blood. I promised to respect her privacy and so will not divulge her name.

An abusive, child-molesting husband and a pregnant teenager daughter with a history of drug abuse are some of her challenges. When I asked why she has lived much longer than most people with AIDS, she said, "It's the good Lord." I asked, "What do you mean, the good Lord?" She replied by pointing to her heart and then to her head. She said, "If I listen to my busy mind, I get angry. If I lead with my heart first, my mind follows the lead and I don't allow myself to get upset."

(Love is patient and thinks no evil)

Love Thinks No Evil

Without a doubt, thinking no evil is the toughest of all challenges. Our monkey-like minds are programmed to strike back, to retaliate, to make others wrong. This is why it is so important to retrain ourselves to become Love's Pilgrim, to start being here for God.

In the above example, the lady with AIDS has struggled not to hate—the hospital, her ex-husband, God, etc.

There is plenty of rage in the human race consciousness. There is lots of support to "sue the bastards." Unfortunately, if we sink to that level of expression, we too are a "bastard."

Are we here on planet earth to learn God's likeness? Is God Love? The best way I know of to get to know "the good Lord" is to love. The "good" is Love. The "Lord" is Law. The law of cause and effect accepts the seed of a bastard as readily as it accepts the seed of Love. And the sun shines on the just and unjust alike. Is there a lesson for us in these examples?

Yesterday I was counseling a suicidal person. His monkey-like repetitive mind was full of depressing thoughts. "No one wants to hire me." "I'm too old." "I am a social misfit." "I don't have any money." "My truck is falling apart." "My leg is bothering me," and on and on. I said to him, "You are right. Those are very depressing thoughts." Then I stated, "Sam, you have two choices. One, to commit suicide; two, to change your mind." "I can't change the way I think or feel," Sam said. I told him, "Yes you can. Love rules the mind and feelings."

I continued, "One way to put this theory into practice is to volunteer your time to help someone worse off than you. By genuinely giving of yourself, your heart will open. Sam, it is not possible to be depressed in the presence of Love. Love is more than a thought. It is more than an emotion. It is the power of God expressing in fullness. God can't do it for you. God can only express Its Love through you. Love requires a cooperative effort.

If we have a fear of rejection, we think we are not good enough. It takes an act of courage to move through the fear. No one else can do it for us." The way out of depression is expression; and that expression is Love.
(Love is unselfishness)

Dr. Thomas Hora (M.D.), author of *Existential Meta-psychiatry*, has had much success with individual and group therapy. Hora said, "Jesus had the right position from the standpoint of intelligent living. He said there is no power but Love; Love is the only power there is; therefore, if you want to be healthy, if you want to be a beneficial presence in the world, you must learn to discipline your thoughts in such a way that they may be prevalently loving thoughts. Should we happen to fall into a situation where we are flooded with unloving thoughts, we can quickly reject them. We must replace them with loving thoughts, and there will be no ill effect. But if we do not live a disciplined mental life, we can become victims of our own unloving thoughts."
(Love thinks no evil)

Think No Evil

The other day on the tennis courts, I was playing men's doubles. On the next court four ladies were playing. One of the ladies had an extraordinarily beautiful body, and I found myself sneaking peeks at her body. Such a healthy and beautiful body. But I disciplined my mind to stay on my game of tennis. I also disciplined my mind to sneak peeks at her when it did not interfere with my tennis game. When does admiration turn to lust? The answer that comes to mind is, when we take the game too seriously—when we become all-consumed by anything other than Love.

(Love does not act unseemly)

Our monkey-mind, or what St. Paul called our carnal mind, is ruled by repetitious lower thoughts. Thoughts that are destructive come from making choices that are less than divine. Thoughts that are constructive are loving thoughts. Love is God; to be God-like is to love. There is a biblical passage that says, "Let this mind be in you, which was also in Christ Jesus" (Philippians 2:5). What does this mean? Jesus frequently said, "It is the Father within that does the work." "The same works which I do, testify concerning me; that the Father has sent me" (John 5:36). "As I hear, I judge; and my judgement is just: Because I seek not mine own will, but the will of the Father which hath sent me" (John 5:30). You may ask, "What does all this mean? I am not Jesus. I do not hear a voice of the 'Father within'!"

What this means to me is, the Father within is God, and God is Love. If I am expressing Love, I am expressing the Father's will. What gets in the way of that is my own ego will. On the tennis court of life, I am by nature competitive. However, I endeavor to be the true sportsman by making the game a fun, loving adventure. When I find I am making winning or losing too important, I change my thoughts to the joy of participation. I express gratitude and kindness. I sincerely compliment my opponents. I try to be kind to myself for making mistakes.

We have it backward—Love is the most enlightened game. The only game to play is learning to express Love. Love is not dependent on the score or the outcome. Love provides the life force—the energy—and how it is spent is up to us.

(Love is kind and seeks not our own lower thoughts, but Godlike thoughts)

Beyond Appearances

This world is dependent on God, and God is Love. Nothing in the world lasts. Some say the world is an illusion, some say it is a reflection of our collective minds. Most certainly, the world is an opportunity to learn the meaning of Love. Divine Love is eternal. We can't possess it, but we can *express* it. To the extent we express Love, we are God-like. To the extent we deny Love, we are Godless . . . we are the fallen child. We fall out of the consciousness of Love.

The Adam and Eve in us is the fallen child. They are our lower thoughts waiting to be redeemed into God-like thoughts. To be born again, we must learn to express what God wants. We macho men born of Adam (as in Adam and Eve) will often sell our souls to possess a beautiful woman's body. We women of Eve will often sell our bodies to the highest bidder for what we want—

security. As children of God, we begin to realize that we are not here to get what we want. We are here for God. What is it that God wants? God wants us, Its children, to resemble Itself. Purely and simply, that self is Love. We are here to express our true identity. Our true identity is more than a human body—it is Love.

We might say, "God, she is beautiful!" or "God, she is awful looking!" Something in us knows, though, that real Love is not perceived in a material way. Love perceives the essence of another, which also is Love. The vibration of Love is constant, everywhere and in everyone. To know Love requires going deeper than the form, for true emotional security is formless. The only lasting security is in God, and God is Love. We need to remind ourselves that we are all created in God's likeness.

The form that Love takes depends on us. One form that we can create out of Love is friendship. But remember that emotional security is not found in form itself; it comes from what we ourselves put into the form we call friendship. I want to tell you a beautiful story of Love in relationships.

A Beautiful Story

A wonderful lady in her seventies gave me permission to share her story but not her name. Let's call her Ruth. Ruth came from a good Protestant background where sexual intercourse was saved for marriage. Unfortunately or fortunately, her husband deserted her and their two small children. When she told her church friends that she was divorcing her missing husband, her friends rejected her. She decided to leave her church. Divorce was considered by them to be sinful under any circumstances.

She managed to raise her children on her salary. Later in life she married a second time, to a man she loved and admired. Soon after their marriage her husband became ill, and she nursed him along for many years until he made his transition. That happened five years ago.

A mysterious thing then happened. Ruth received a phone call from a college boyfriend. The man, now in his seventies, had been trying to locate her for several years, and finally he learned where she was through mutual friends. The two still had strong feelings for each other even after more than 50 years, and they agreed to meet. Of course, they both looked older, but they seemed to pick up right where they left off. He too had been widowed for over five years.

At Ruth's age she had not been looking for sex or even wanting it. ''That notion totally disappeared until we met again,'' she said. ''But it was clear that the same spark of attraction was between us that was there years ago. Not only did I have a deep, soul-felt Love for this man, but I wanted to be with him in the most intimate way, as he did with me.''

I can't wait to share with you the rest of what Ruth told me. Her story is what prompted me to discuss the subject of sex. We all have so many different beliefs about sex. There is beauty and joy in any act when Love is present.

(Love is kind)

Here is what she says:

"This is when a new realization about the act of intercourse came to me as clearly as a bell. I wonder how many others have had this enlightenment. It is so simple and yet I do not recall reading it anywhere or hearing anyone express it. For the first time I realized that the act of sex, the one which our Creator fashioned to be the way the race is propagated, was carefully planned by Him, our beloved Creator, as was every other creation He made. The wonderful, heightened climax two people reach during this experience is simply the physical way they are expressing their deep, soul-felt love for each other. It must be felt physically because we are physical beings. To feel it on a mental, emotional and even spiritual level also makes Love feel complete. We must give thanks to God for planning so beautifully the way we can express physical feelings for each other, when we truly love."

Ruth goes on to say, "It is very sad to me that sex has been degenerated to be thought of as an animal act. True, sexual intercourse is of the flesh, but we are Spirit expressing as flesh and blood. The planned magnetic attraction God put into us for the one we are to Love in a spiritual way is confused with the purely physical attraction. Or else it is the other way around; a physical attraction is confused with a spiritual Love.

"I know there is a plenty of sex going on out there, but I wish people could have the experience which I have finally had, that of a sexual relationship with someone I Love deeply in an emotional, mental and spiritual way and now have the marvelous experience and privilege of expressing it in a physical way."

(Love never fails. Love is kind, generous, unselfish and courteous)

Thank you, Ruth. I wonder what *Dr.* Ruth's comments would be on this subject? . . .

Again, the enlightened choice is Love. The promise is, if we seek heaven first, all else will be given to us. If God is Love, then heaven must be Love's haven. Yet, Love is more than a refuge. It is a consciousness that is everywhere to be realized. Our intention is the key. Are we coming from our heart center first? Do our thoughts embody our highest concept of Love?

PART II

LOVE: HOW IT WORKS

LOVE works in unlimited ways. It reveals itself to us as it is expressed. It is a universal principle, a divine quality that brings light, lightheartedness, Spirit into our full expression. It is the central power that energizes and pervades everything. Love cannot be defined but can be described and known to those of us who use it.

How Love Works

Each of us examines, analyzes, and realizes Love according to our belief, feelings and experience. We may differentiate Love in terms of brotherly, child-like, neighborly, spousal, romantic, unconditional and divine Love. Our hearts yearn to express Love in fullness. Our self-limited access to Divine Mind comes from a belief in separation from our Source. How it works is most easily described in terms of relationships. Numerous examples of how Love works and what is required of us to be faithful to this God-like quality follow.

A Disease Called Touchiness

Professor Drummond said, "There is a disease called touchiness. A disease which, in spite of its innocent name, is one of the greatest sources of restlessness in the world. Touchiness, when it becomes chronic, is a morbid condition of the inward disposition. It is self-love inflamed to the acute point. The cure is to shift the yoke to some other place. To let men and things touch us through some new and perhaps as yet unused part of our nature. To become meek and lowly in heart while the old nature is becoming numb from want of use."

Does Love Bind or Set Free?

A good basic question to ask ourselves is, "Does Love bind or set us free?" For example, often when we get married or enter into a relationship with a significant other, we make vows or promises that bind us. Is that Love? When we choose an employment that is something we love doing and commit to work so many hours a week, is that binding? Is Love a freedom from that which binds? Is unconditional Love a freedom that has no restrictions, no thing that binds?

I was asked yesterday by a very nice young lady, "Aren't you happy that you do not have an eight-to-five job?" My immediate response was "yes." But after a moment's reflection, I felt a need to tell her that when I worked eight-to-five I was also happy. I guess if we are happy, the binding does not hurt. Don't you agree? Let's examine relationships for what hurts and what heals.

Tempers Are Provoked: Relationship Hurts

QUESTION: How do I get along with my girlfriend who makes her stuff so important that she interrupts me? She scolds me.

The male's presenting problem: I was spilling my guts out to her while driving down the highway. I am very disturbed that my ex-wife makes it very difficult for me to see my only son. All of a sudden, out of the blue, my girlfriend interrupted me. She scolded me for having one of her audio cassette tapes on the floor of the car. She interrupted me as I was spilling my guts. She made me wrong for having her $10 tape on the floor. I got angry about her insensitivity and used some language she does not approve of. I can't understand her.

The female's presenting problem: He does not respect my stuff. When I saw my cassette tape on the floor, I imagined he threw it down when he was angry. He knows I am particular about my stuff. I gave him some rules when he came to live with me. I like my house neat.

The drama: He is not speaking to her. She calls him from work. He is still angry. He reiterates the problem. He can't understand how she could be so crass as to interrupt him and shame him over some trivial cassette tape. She asked for forgiveness but did not sound convincing to him. She has a pressure job that demands her attention while she slips in personal phone calls. He is not interested in her feeble appeal for forgiveness. He wants understanding and he is very insistent. A third party pulls out a book that helps clarify what "understanding" is.

(Love is kind and humble)

We offer this input to the male: "Understanding requires more than the intellect, it requires an open heart." He is not ready to open his heart. So he has no hope of truly understanding. His attempt at understanding is prejudiced by his belief that his emotional stuff was much more important than her stuff. He was bent on proving her wrong.

(Love does not puff up oneself, or seek her own)

RECOMMENDATION: We all can make our stuff very important. It makes little difference if our stuff is emotional, intellectual or physical. We are so interested at times in our stuff that we shame and blame others. We can become so righteous about our stuff that we are blind to Love.

It takes courage to surrender our stuff. We think that we will lose our identity. We all tend to identify with our problems and with our things.

Want to heal the feeling of separation? Identify first

with Love. True Love heals. Righteous indignation separates us.

(Love is good temper)

Tough Love: Behaves Unseemly

An AIDS victim, who admitted the frequent use of drugs and promiscuous sex as a teenager and young adult, is most disturbed. He is disturbed with his parents who are permissive, thereby enabling his younger brother to follow in his footsteps. The parents are recoving alcoholics and legalized drug users. He refers to his family as dysfunctional. Tough Love is his solution. He feels estranged and has suffered much from his own dysfunctional ways. He feels his life slipping away and wants to right what he sees wrong in his family. If he gets tough with his father and mother, maybe he can prevent them from supporting or enabling his brother the alcoholic. A noble idea to fix someone else. Just ask me.

I tried to help this young man, the AIDS victim, by telling him a story of how I demanded change in a brother for all the ''right'' reasons and all I got was resentment. The real resentment was in myself, but I projected it on my brother. Fortunately, God gave me an opportunity to see my resentment and to seek forgiveness. It felt as if a heavy burden was removed from my shoulders. It lasted for a day or two. I went from criticizing my brother (which was a burden) to a state of grace that allowed me to unconditionally love him. And from there I wanted to fix him, to rescue him, and I became burdened again. It took me a year to understand what I had done.

Love Seeks Not Her Own

My desire to help the AIDS victim backfired a week later when he called me and in very strong language told me to mind my own business. In this kind of situation, it is best not to ever contradict his feelings. He believes in "tough" Love. Within three minutes I really got his hurt and his anger now directed at me. From there we settled down into a peaceful conversation that lasted half an hour. He was right; I had suggested to him an alternative way. He did not ask me to verbalize to him my feeling about what he shared. Little did I know he would take my suggestion as a threat. I had even supported my feelings with scripture. (That makes it sound more spiritual.) I thank God I was not addicted to my suggestion, my feelings—or to scripture. I did not have to prove my way was better. (Too often, I can get stuck in being self-righteous.)

God gave me the courage to hang in there, and through the upset and hurt came Love. I trust he no longer has to hold a grievance toward me or I toward him. I call this courageous feeling from God, soft Love. Only God can give us the power to heal the wounds in relationships. Love is not imposing our beliefs or demanding that our position be recognized as right. If we do this, we become victims of our own pride, and we lose the close feeling that only Love can give to us.

(Love is kind)

Respect

How do you feel about respect? Is it an aspect of Love? Is it something you expect, or demand, from others? Is it something you earn? Is it something you give?

My soon-to-be 80-year-old mother was telling me about respect. I have had the wonderful privilege of getting reacquainted with her by living in her home for a while and sharing our feelings, beliefs and values. How marvelous it is to get reacquainted. It amazes me to see the number of people of all ages who just pop in on her. They like to confide in her. She is a good active listener. She does not allow her beliefs or feelings to get in the way of someone else sharing theirs. She does not have to agree or disagree openly. She listens intently and understands the message. She can be equally stubborn in her point of view. So can I. Maybe that is a character flaw. In any event, we are both characters. What does our character have to do with respect?

My mother grew up in an era where she was taught to respect her elders. Most of us in the Judeo/Christian culture were taught to honor our parents. In today's world we often blame our parents for our birth defects and other things. We say our problems today are a result of parental abuse—physical, mental or emotional. Is finding fault with our parents respectful? Can we honor behavior we disapprove of?

Mother was sharing with me this story: A young girl around eight years of age was playing a game with her at the dining room table. It might have been a card game—Mom does love her card games. The child stuck her tongue out and gave Mom a raspberry (a noise with her tongue). She was being disrespectful to Mom. Mom proceeded to inform her that you cannot do that to adults, that it is disrespectful. "Do not ever do that in my house again," she warned the child. The underlying message is, "I'll teach you to be a lady." A noble idea. Although, I wonder if, as adults, we would perhaps benefit from respecting the feelings of others, in this case a child.

Teach Respect by Respecting

If we will not allow a child to stick their tongue out at us, what are we doing? Are we being disrespectful to their feelings? Are we able to appreciate their feelings? Or are we endeavoring to intimidate them into becoming a lady? Are we able to give respect when we feel another is making fun of us? Or do we take ourselves too seriously? It is easier to tell someone to lighten up or to "chill out" than to understand and respect their feelings.

   (Love does not puff up oneself)

Truth

Most of us think the way to get respect, or teach respect, is by using force; "I'll make something out of you," we feel. Do we really want to make children over in our image and likeness? The image we are striving to make is Love. Do we really want to deny feelings, our own or those of others? Is not Truth to be acknowledged, expressed and recognized from moment to moment? There is nothing greater than Truth, and no Truth greater than Love.

(Love rejoices in Truth)

Can we respect other people's feelings if we do not respect our own? Do our feelings come from treasured beliefs that bypass the heart of spontaneity?

Disrespect for Feeling

QUESTION: How can I understand my wife? She had me thrown out of the house by the police. I had no warning. I did not even know there was a problem.

The male's point of view: We had been married for five years. I took a week off work to help her with our first child. I thought all was well. Without a clue I was evicted from my home and accused of abuse.

The female's point of view: He was abusive to me and my baby. I had no choice but to throw him out, to protect myself and my baby and end the marriage. I just pretended that everything was OK. For several years I have been hiding my true feelings.

(Love is sincere, even about feelings)

The drama: The male was very competitive and expected the female to dote on him. If she wanted a relationship with him, she must be interested in the things he liked. Participating in or watching sports events was high on his agenda. In any disagreement, he would almost always win. A competitive male, a dominant male, gets his way by shouting or intimidating.

(Love vaunteth not itself)

The female: Her idea of Love was doting and pretending to like all the things that interested him. She would mask her true feelings. In her attempt to feel good, she would eat and spend in excess, and use her secret charge account.

(Love seeks not her own)

Character defects: Male self-indulgent, and needs to win and dominate. Female overly indulgent, timid, shy and deceitfully self-indulgent.

RECOMMENDATION: Go into counseling to discover any character flaws that you might have. We can't change others, but we can change ourselves. Love is not being dominant or inconsiderate of others' thoughts and feelings. Neither is Love being timid or deceitful about your feelings. The self-indulgence we don't like in others is actually within ourselves. The dominator gets dominated. Love, however, is free of dominance. Love is free to give. There is no pretense in Love; Truth prevails.

Don't spend much time on the problem. Learn to identify with Love in all your relationships.

Love Is Patient

A young boy tested his mother's patience, and she passed the test of Love. I was leaving my home and was greeted by the seven-year-old boy who lives next door. James is his name. James said to me that he was running away from home. "Don't worry, I won't go in your house. I'll just stay here in your yard." I was puzzled as James hostilely took off and entered his home. At my feet was a bag of his clothes and a few toys. I picked up the bag and walked to his front door. I rang the bell and in a few moments his mother appeared. I explained that James was running away from home. She said she knew; "He came home to get his bike. I could kill him!"

I was concerned about her attitude, but I knew she was just expressing her feelings. She is a caring mother who had taken time out to play woofer ball with her two sons just an hour before this incident. James did tell me the reason he was running away from home: At home he could not do everything he wanted to do, because his mother gave him restrictions.

James' mother was patient and allowed her son to experience what it is like to run away from home. She could verbalize her frustrations to me; she did not bottle them up. Stored anger is abusive to the one holding it and to the one it is directed at. There is a definite mind-body connection. Anger is prompted by someone, or something happening, that we do not like.

James' mother did not direct her anger at her son. She was patient enough to allow him to run away from home and experience the results of his actions. She was also unhappy with him and he knew it.

(Love beareth all things)

How wonderful it is to give each other some distance to cool down, to chill out. The next day I met James and his five-year-old brother, Matthew. They were outside my home chasing each other with squirt guns. I asked James to come in, and Matthew followed. I told them I was writing a book about Love. I asked them what Love means to them. Here is the answer I got.

"Love is marriage, sex. Love is friendship. Love is kissing, being together, dancing, having a girlfriend. Love is helping."

I asked James: "How did you feel when you ran away?" He said, "Angry, and that's not Love."

How do you feel now that you're back home? "I feel sad, and sad has some Love in it."

I thanked them for their help, and as they were leaving, James turned quickly around and said, "THE SPECIALEST KIND OF LOVE IN THE WORLD IS THE LOVE OF EVERYTHING."

(Love endureth all things)

Wow, was I impressed! This thing called Infinite Intelligence was speaking through the mouths of babes. "Seek and you will find; knock and it will be opened unto you." The same power that gives Itself as Intelligence gives Itself to us as Love. How marvelous it is to recognize Love and to understand Its value at any age.

Hate is destructive. Love is instructive and constructive in and of Itself.

Love Is Instructive

There is a spiritual Law that is as certain and exacting as the law of mathematics. It acts according to our belief. It is what psychologists call the subjective or unconscious mind. Putting hate, revenge or uncertainty into it will perpetuate more of the same. It mirrors back to us our thoughts, feelings and beliefs.

It is an instructive law. What you sow is what you reap. Put anger in, get anger out. (Or as a computer buff says, "GIGO—garbage in, garbage out.") What goes around, comes around. This law of cause and effect is perfect. If we believe in an eye for an eye, we believe in retribution. We demand justice. We demand respect.

Whatever we demand will be demanded of us. Whatever we give will be given to us. We do not have to do anything to anyone. *"The result is in the cause itself."* This karmic law has no choice but to respond in kind. This law is not limited by time or space. We often suffer in this life for the negative way we have treated ourselves or others. If life is forever, this law of cause and effect is also forever.

We brought some baggage with us into this world. Call it, if you like, DNA coding on the soul. When we leave this world we will take with us the unresolved effects. Kill someone and be killed. Love someone and be loved. It is that simple and exact. Two plus two always equals four in any language. It does not matter that we are ignorant of mathematics or how the law works. It works anyway.

Suffering gets our attention eventually. It will invite us to understand. What are we to understand? That Love is the answer.

Love is the law of our being. To know Love is to know God. To know Love is to know Self. To know Love is to know one another at our core.

Simple test: Withhold love, and it is painful. Hold a grudge, and we feel separated. This is the instructive Law of Love. Give Love freely in all our words, deeds and activities, and we feel more interconnected to the whole of life.

Can we forgive a person or a God for not giving us the license to do anything we want? The answer lies in free choice. Choose to live the principle of Divine Love. That is the only true freedom from the confines of our beliefs, dogmas and doctrines. It does not matter if we are agnostic, atheistic or religious; the principle still works. Its application is up to us.

If we make our belief in anything more important than expressing Love, we miss the mark . . . the mark of completion, the mark of wholeness, the mark of joy.

The seven-year-old boy is *our* story. We get angry, and we leave home. We are angry; we have a strong belief in self-importance. We journey back home. We are sad because we think we have something to lose. We think we have to please Mom. We get home, appreciate what we have, and we are happy.

A broken heart comes from taking something or someone too seriously. Pain is a clue that we are not in harmony with the Divine Principle called Love.

Mom Held a Grievance

My dear mother gave us this terrific example of holding a grievance for all the ''right'' reasons and the benefit of giving it up. Mother shared her Love and home with a man for 17 years. We affectionately called him Uncle Bill. When he died, his son Dave came to claim all his father's belongings. He took things that Mom and Bill purchased together that held sentimental value to her. He also took items that were hers alone. Mom said nothing at the time. She was definitely angry and held a grievance for many years until she heard that Bill's son Dave was on his deathbed. She decided to call him.

Divine Love prompted her to forgive him. She needed

to get this pain off her chest. She immediately felt better. Divine Love is always prompting us to express ''It.''

Love is the Truth of being. It is real. It is forever. Grievances evaporate in the presence of Love. Grievances are transitory. They are something we made up. Grievances are something we justify according to our beliefs.

Love is a Divine Presence that always *Is*. Like the law of mathematics, *It* was always there for humankind to discover and use. Mom found It in a genuine act of forgiveness. Thanks, Mom, for permitting me to share the story. It is our story in Truth and the consequences of our thoughts. We are no different from Mom. Love as Law applies equally to all of us.

(Love thinks no evil, and Love never fails)

Love Can't Be Bargained For

The problem in writing about a principle such as Love is that words can only point or suggest. The symbol is not the thing Itself. Most words also convey the chance of an opposite. Most of us would say the opposite of Love is hate. But, in reality, no thing can oppose Love. Love is no-thing to oppose. Love endures all things, and nothing can destroy true Love. This invisible, yet recognizable, quality within ourselves never changes. Our moods change, our feelings change, our bodies change—yet there is something that stays the same. We may pour our

Love or energy into all kinds of things. The things themselves change, yet Love can never be created or destroyed. It just is the life force within us.

A person who hates is hurting. Under the hate is fear—fear of loss: loss of life, loss of relationship, loss of property, loss of job, etc. Hate and fear may blind us to Love. Are we ready to give ourselves to something greater than fear, greater than self-importance? Give ourselves first to Love. As we become able to express true Love, fear and hate disappear. They vanish.

Love is an invisible presence that is always there, a no-thing. Like the principles of mathematics, you can't see it. It is no-thing. Yet, it is always there waiting to be discovered and used. Love is always the correct answer. Love will reduce fear and hate within us to nothing. That is the paradox. How can a no-thing such as Love reduce fear and hate to nothing? Maybe we don't need to know how Love works. Maybe it is enough to choose it, to make it more important. Love is its own reward. It liberates from fear and hate. Love is a gift, not a possession. Love liberates us from ignorance, from the confines of self-importance. It restores us to the light of God within us, as us. Jesus called this light the Father within. Christians call it the Christ. Psychology calls it compassion. Joseph Campbell calls it bliss.

Life Is a Carnival
("You Choose the Ride")

Some of the time in the carnival of life we have a bumper-car mentality. We are looking to hit or bump or to run from hits or bumps.

One time I went to a carnival-of-life weekend experience. It was run by some psychologists. I was going through a mid-life change and was looking forward to learning more about myself. I discovered lots of things, and it was a most productive weekend.

So often we project guilt or fear onto others. Usually onto those close to us. Blaming and shaming are a bumper-car mentality. Here is what happened that weekend.

The Bumper-Car Mentality

The drama: After lunch many of us decided to take a yoga class. There were many classes to choose from in each period of the day, and my wife chose a different class. The yoga instructor began with an exercise to speed up our digestive processes, and I was paired off with an attractive young lady. Your partner was asked to massage your stomach area. I became fearful that I would expel gas, which would be embarrassing with a perfect stranger. I don't think anyone is a stranger to expelling gas, so I was making myself guilty for being human. I wanted to be something special, a human being without gas.

(Love suffereth all things, even the state of being human)

The next experience was even more embarrassing. As we reversed roles, while rubbing her stomach I became sexually aroused. What if she noticed? Here I am, a married person who should have sexual feelings only for his wife. I experienced fear—fear of doing wrong, fear of getting caught, fear of breaking up my marriage. God help me! What am I to do? I left the class feeling guilty.

Then I heard some voices and laughter coming from another group exiting their class. My wife's laughter was apparent and I could hear her conversing with a male who had a deep, carrying voice. I just knew she must be doing something wrong to be having so much fun!

Rather than bumping her car, I decided to sort out my feelings in private. She thought I was being antisocial when I opted not to take the next class. Thank God, I came to the realization that I was projecting my guilt onto her.

It is a real blessing when we can see our own character flaws. My urge to strike out and accuse her melted away. And I could forgive myself for having sexual feeling toward another. Fear is the bumper-car of life. Love cushions the hit to ourselves or others.

(Love is kind to ourself and others)

Fear Projected

We often project our fear onto someone else, real or imagined. A married man had been sexually active at his place of employment. Later this man became very upset with a teacher at his church. He ordered the minister to have a male teacher in the church thrown out. The minister, of course, asked him why. He said it was because his wife had an alleged affair with the visiting teacher. The complaining husband was not interested in examining his own character flaws. He was not sensitive to his wife's needs in their relationship. He became incensed with another man who was just like him. He too was sexually active outside of marriage. The husband was striking out at the other fellow who was not unlike himself.

(Love does not think evil of ourself or others)

We all have character flaws that cast shadows onto others, don't we? The husband knew something was not right within himself. We all project our fear on others, real or imagined, don't we?

We live in a society that is quickly changing. National boundaries are giving way to a one-world mentality. In order to live peacefully, only Love can dispel the fear. To have an understanding heart requires us to be introspective. What belief are we holding onto that is more important than Love? Can we forgive our own character flaws as well as the flaws of other characters?

(Love is generous)

The Ferris Wheel Experience

The ferris wheel of life goes around and around, like the second-hand on a clock, or the seasons of a year. We've bought our ticket for the duration of the ride. The passengers sharing our chair may be special to us. Maybe one of them is our significant other.

The ferris wheel of life moving up and around, back and forth, stopping abruptly or smoothly, is a metaphor for our relationships. As the ferris wheel approaches the high point, is it a hair-raising experience coming from fear, or is it a peak experience realized out of Love?

My 83-year-old aunt (we'll call her Ruby) had a special relationship with her daughter Ann. However, a time came when Ann became angry with her mother for showing favoritism to a grandson who did not deserve it. The grandson, Bill, was always getting into trouble. Ann would not speak to her mother. She withheld her verbal communication from her mother, trying to force her to change her ways.

However, Ruby would not conform to her daughter's demands. She felt she had a right to spend her money on her grandson if she wished. Ruby felt her daughter was more interested in her money than in her. Aunt Ruby was troubled by all this. When I suggested she try to talk with her daughter, she said, "Absolutely not. It would break my heart if she rejected me again."

(She behaved unseemly, ruled by fear)

This drama, or one like it, emerges in every family. And it keeps repeating itself. It goes around and around and around.

The karmic wheel of repetitious behavior *can* be used constructively, though. We all create special relationships. The trouble is, we put great stock in making it special. *Our* child, *our* spouse, *our* parent, *our* friend, *our* house, *our* money, *our* feelings. When we get frightened on the ferris wheel of life, it is often because we are fearful of loss. We might call it a Love loss. But if we put true Love in all our relationships, the ride becomes joyful.

Aunt Ruby's fear of rejection was keeping her from venturing forth to start a conversation with her daughter. Underneath the pain of rejection is an incredible force called Love. It can be neither created nor destroyed. It is the only thing that can heal the pain of separation. When we find the Love in our heart that we have denied, the gift of Love brings us to a state of bliss. We have a blissful experience, a peak experience that has reached the top of the ferris wheel.

When we feel the pain of separation, what are we trusting in? What have we made more special than Love? In Aunt Ruby's case, it took a tragedy to bring her into verbal communication with her daughter. Cousin Ann's child came down with a terminal illness. Ruby's grandchild was in trouble; Ruby's daughter was falling apart. The severity of the situation caused them to speak to one another, giving them an opportunity to resolve the conflict in their souls. They learned that it is all right to have different points of view; just don't make them more important than Love.

(Love is kind)

Answer of a Five-Year-Old

As I was writing these words, a wonderful five-year-old girl came to the door to tell me something. She was playing house with her three-year-old cousin. I had previously spent time with them to observe their relationship, so I asked each of them about Love. Here is the message the older child sang to me:

"I got one and you got two. It makes no difference, 'cause I Love you." A five-year-old child knows LOVE is the answer.

(Love is unselfish)

Can't Win for Losing

"I'll be damned if I do, I'll be damned if I don't." Have you ever found yourself in a no-win situation? You can't please the other person no matter what you do.

My dear mother, after 25 years of being a dutiful housewife, divorced my father. It was a traumatic experience for all our family members at the time. My father demanded a lot from my mother, and she would not challenge his authority on anything. She believed it was not her right. Underneath that belief was a fear of insecurity that our society bred into women of her generation. Women usually were not prepared to be more than housewives and mothers. ''What would happen to me and the children if I spoke up and challenged his authority?'' she asked herself.

In dominant-passive relationships, such as boss vs. employee, one spouse over the other, leader vs. follower, guru vs. student, we sometimes find ourselves in a no-win situation.

In my mother's case, she couldn't have a speck of dust on the furniture, had to have the potatoes on when Dad arrived, etc. He insisted she be dressed in a certain way to impress his business friends. Yet he would manage to find fault with *something*.

Several years after the divorce, Mother moved to another state, found a new circle of friends, and literally became a new person. Mom desired to work. She knew she must do something constructive to earn a living. She moved to the state of Washington with a male companion who introduced her to fishing. She bought some property on Clear Lake and opened a fishing and hunting business. Mom says, ''I always find courage to do what is important to me. I just fell into the resort business.'' A very demanding business gave her a way to serve, to give of herself once again.

She no longer lived a lifestyle where she suppressed her true feelings for the good of the family. She was now more vocal, independent and relieved . . . relieved from the pressure of living with a demanding perfectionist. She would sometimes refer to my dad as "his highness." Have you ever tried to please someone who is unhappy? You come to their rescue and find they project their unhappiness on you. What do you do with another person's unhappiness projected at you?

(Love is sincere)

A No-Win Situation

A young lady in her early thirties called early this morning, and she was troubled. Her fiance had to appear in court to complete his divorce. They both had been working long hours and had spent a restless night with little sleep. She wanted help in making a decision. On the one hand, her fiance wanted her to attend his court appearance with him for moral support. On the other hand, he did not want her to attend if her presence would be a liability to him. She had never met his wife, and they were concerned with protocol within the court system. Concern is often a disguised fear.

"It is better to make choices from Love than from fear," I said. "I won't attempt to make your choice. Look at what you are basing your choice on."

"What do you mean?" she said.

"You are stymied in your no-win situation because you are trying to please your fiance. He wants you there for support, but is afraid your presence in the court might hurt his case. You can't decide because you fear his rejection. So what is the answer? What does your heart tell you?''

"I really want to be there to support him. I took the day off from work. I guess I'll go." She made her choice based on Love.

Some ministers say to turn your worries over to God. I don't believe God is interested in worries or fear. But I believe the ministers are right about not taking ourselves too seriously.

(Love is not fearful, Love is sincere)

Can we possibly follow the example of the young child, the child who said, "I got one and you got two, it makes no difference, 'cause I Love you"? God knows how seriously we take property settlements, parenting plans, divorces, and each other. But Love leaves the outcome up to the Almighty. We do our part as an instrument of Love. The outcome of the young lady's choice was wonderful. She met and established good rapport with her fiance's ex-wife. She was also a calm comfort to her fiance and the court did not care that she was there.

(Love is good temper)

To Hell with Worries
To Heaven with Love

On the surface that sounds like a flippant remark: "To hell with worries, to heaven with Love." It's flippant because we all worry, and it is wonderful because we all love. What gives a mother, a spouse, an employee, a student the courage to speak their hearts? By courage, I mean a clear mind guided by the heart. An intelligent choice goes beyond the intellect, resulting in an inspired choice . . . a choice not made out of fear, a choice not made out of cold intellect alone, a choice not made out of false pride. Courageous choice is the most wonderful kind of choice. If God is Love, and if we are expressing Love, we are realizing what God is. That truly is wonderful!

(Love rejoices in truth)

I asked a 70-year-old woman who has no problem speaking her mind, "What is Love?" She said, "Love is what you get if you give."

Eighty-year-old Mom just read to me, "Love has no direction, no up or down. It has no gravity." Love truly has no borders—geographical, cultural, political, religious or otherwise. Love has no hidden agenda. Love makes no demands. Love is not possessive. Love is a gift. Love is an unlimited bank account of spiritual essence. Love cannot be overdrawn.

(Love never fails)

Love Is Patient

So often in our fast-paced world that we have created, we get impatient with ourselves or others. An old-time expression is, he or she has "blown a fuse." If Love is our energy source, it's as though negativity interrupts the natural flow. Not many people like to be around an angry or disturbed person. His or her behavior can be frightening. But when Love is flowing, fear is cast out.

The other day in the supermarket, a middle-aged, well-built, large black male cashier was very rude to the person in front of me in line. He had demanded in a loud disturbing voice, "Give me those cans." After the customer left, the cashier volunteered to tell me that this man has been coming in for years. "His brain is in his buttocks. He refuses to let go of the cans, and so I can't scan them for pricing," he said.

(Love is not easily provoked)

Can We Change?

How about the tennis player who always gets upset with himself if he makes a poor shot? No one likes to play with him. I asked such a person why he is so hard on himself. He answered, "I've always been that way." Sometimes his anger or impatience carries over to blaming his partner. The almighty spirit of competition gets in the way of true enjoyment. Happiness may be our inalienable right, but choosing to express it is a matter of determination. Competition is fine. The problem is we take ourselves too seriously. We have taught ourselves to be competitive—to win, no matter what the cost. But we can train ourselves to become happier, more loving human beings.

(Love is good temper)

Three Steps to Change Ourselves

The *first step* toward change is *recognizing* that the Divine urge within ourselves is Love. *Having awareness* of what is required of us to express Love is the *second step*. The *third step* is *expressing* Love in our thoughts, deeds and activities.

Perfect Love

Perfect Love often requires us to give up our *perfected* idea of who we are. Ever get upset or angry with yourself for forgetting or losing something?

A dear friend drove a long distance to join us in the celebration of Mother's 80th birthday. When it came time to give her his carefully chosen birthday card, he could not find it. During the five minutes it took him to find it, his blood pressure rose. He got so angry he could have put his fist through the houseboat window. However, he was too much a ''perfect'' gentleman to allow himself to do that.

(Love is kind, even to oneself)

Many of us take personal pride in having a good memory. We get angry with ourselves for not being able to find a birthday card we bought and put away for later use. We hold ourselves to "perfect" standards that fail to match our reality. God, teach us to laugh at ourselves! **(Love is good temper)**

The "perfect" idea of the thin young lady on the houseboat was to be even thinner. "Oh," she tormented herself, "if I could only be a size five instead of a size seven!" But size five would have resulted in malnutrition, in my (in)expert opinion. **(Love thinks kindly of oneself.)**

Love the Actor

A dear friend of mine told me that he did not *like* his mother although he loved her. It sounds like a dichotomy —opposing points of view. A teacher once put it this way: "Always love the actors, not the act." In other words, the true impulse behind every thought, deed and activity is Spirit. Spirit is Love Itself. The ways in which we each differentiate the Spirit depend on our beliefs, our hopes, what we image as important. Our choices often distort the real impact of Love's true nature. The act does not resemble the true impulse as it arose from its Source. It's like singing off-key.

What we cherish in our material, emotional or intellectual life is the act, the baggage, the air of self-importance, the perfect figure, the ugly duckling syndrome, etc. The act is energy in form. We, the actors, put energy into something to give it expression. The author puts energy into writing, the surfer into surfing. That creative energy is Love. The form the energy takes will pass away, because the form is always transitory. Books rot, surfers die, and self-importance fades away.

Each of us actors is motivated by Love which is eternal. We must learn to seek and cherish that which is eternal and put less emphasis on the temporal things. Love is real. Love is our essential nature. We can best identify with others through Love, not through transitory things. Love never changes, and it is the force that brings to light what Spirit is. We Love Pilgrims know that Love is not definable, yet it is recognizable. The form we give to Love resembles: patience, kindness, generosity, humility, courtesy, unselfishness, good temper, sincerity. Love is never: egotistical, frightening, thinking evil, joyful in inequity, or easily provoked. We choose Love because we know it never fails. Mother Teresa says it this way: "Love is a fruit in season at all times, and within the reach of every hand."

A Perfect Love Affair

A young engaged couple planned the perfect moonlight love affair in the woods above the lake. Then everything went wrong. Use your own imagination. They even argued about the kind of animal that rolled by them on the steep incline. I suspect the animal lost its footing while laughing at these two. Here they were, trying so hard to make "perfect" Love on a rocky, unstable hill. Their failed attempt at perfect sex climaxed in laughter. What a wonderful way to release an ideal picture that did not materialize. When we take ourselves too seriously, we are short-circuiting the potential to laugh, to love, to be happy, to heal.

Test the Theory

The premise of this book is that Spirit is God, that God is Love, and to know God is to live, to be, to realize, to express Love. There are some who would say we, as humans, could never get to know Love, or to know God. Only God's "perfect" Son could be like Him. The rest of us can't be "perfect." Therefore, redemption is beyond us. There are some who are not interested in redemptive Love or anything that borders on religion. I can understand both points of view.

Here is the challenge to both religious and nonreligious people. To prove the theory of true Love, one must be-live-it. No one can do it for us. It must be done through us. Love is the universal religion and the most practical answer we can realize.

PART III

LOVE: WHAT IT DOES

LOVE: what it does is continuously give of Itself to all. Love needs an outlet. Humankind is an outlet in potential. To the extent that we understand and express what Love truly is, we are redeemed by It. This infinite Intelligence we call Love operates according to divine Law. It contains all knowledge, all wisdom, all knowing. Love can only reveal Its secrets through our receptivity to It. Love expands our awareness, our creativity and enhances our relationships as we express It. That is how It works.

Professor Henry Drummond, whom I introduced at the beginning of this book, was not afraid to voice his opinion. Yet he always remained a gentleman. His teaching of science and religion was on the cutting edge of his day. He taught that all is God. Understanding and application of natural law is what science is about, is it not? Exploring the very nature of reality and the laws pertaining to it. Similarly, getting to know God and expressing God's will is the highest form of spiritual revelation. Religion is compatible with science, and science with religion. Both science and religion explore the allness of life. God is Life in substance and form. God's Love creates everything out of Itself. Itself is Love.

Henry would tell his students, "The final test of religion at the great assize [court of law] is not religiousness, but Love. Not what I have *done*, not what I have *believed*, not what I have *achieved*. But how I have *Loved* . . . How many prodigals [erring sons and daughters] are kept out of the kingdom of God, by the unlovely character of those who profess to be inside."

Nothing Happens by Chance

Drummond as a man of science explained the law of cause and effect in terms of human potential. "The reward of being gentle is to become more gentle. The reward of being liberal is to become more liberal. The reward of controlling temper is to become more sweet-tempered. The penalty of being hard is to become hardened, of being unforgiving is to become cruel. . . . Nothing happens in the world by chance. There is no perhaps in nature. There is a cause for everything that we see, or feel, or hear."

Another great teacher who synthesized science, religion and philosophy was Ernest Holmes. Holmes, in his book *Can We Talk to God?* states: "How can there be an acceptance of a greater good, unless its spiritual significance rises through our mental equivalents to reach the level of that good? If we are still submerged in doubt and fear, in uncertainty and dread, shall not these monsters need first to be slain before peace and confidence can be gained?"

Change: an Inside Job

Change in our behavior is an inside job. No one else is going to do it for us. It must be done through our very own self. Drummond enjoyed reading Ralph Waldo Emerson, and both of them had a profound belief in the human will. He also enjoyed the works of Spinoza, who said: "It is so much the more our duty, not, like the advocate of the evil spirit, always to keep our eyes fixed upon the nakedness and weakness of our nature, but rather to seek out all those perfections through which we can make good our claims to a likeness to God."

Drummond thought that the greatest challenge of his generation was the need for a much broader scriptural idea of God.

"We think of God up there. There is no such thing as up there. What is up there tonight will be down there in twelve hours from this time. Where is God if He is not back there in time or up there in space? Where is He? He is in you. It is God that worketh in you."

Most people today understand the omnipresence of God. Yet some people still believe that the only inspired words are in the Bible. What could be more inspirational than God as Love expressing through us? The point is: *What Love does has to be done through us.*

The apostle Paul stated a profound truth this way, "Love is the fulfilling of the law." What law? Let us ask a man of science—Professor Drummond. "Nothing that happens in the world happens by chance. God is a God of order. Everything is arranged upon definite principles,

and never at random. . . . Character is governed by
law. Happiness is governed by law. . . . Realize it tho-
roughly: it is a methodical, not accidental, world [law].
. . . Effects require causes.''
  Form follows thought as night follows day. ''If a housewife turns out a good cake, it is the result of a sound
recipe, carefully applied.'' What we give our internal attention to becomes our outer experience. Sometimes I'll
find in my internal dialog that I have created in the
privacy of my mind a fight, a conflict, a battle. ''Stop,''
I say to myself, and change the internal dialog to something I consider in line with the Principle of Love. The
Principle of Love is also a Presence. Transforming our
minds requires our interest and certainly our attention.
God works through us.

Example of How Spirit Works through Us

A 92-year-old Religious Healing Practitioner, whose
name was Gertrude N., explained it this way to me.
''Spirit as Love gives us a perfect impulse of pure Love.
This impulse is a creative urge to express our lives fully
and completely. In order to do that, our basic need for
air, water, food and shelter must be met. How we interpret and use this creative urge is up to us. If we have an
urge to be prosperous and we rob banks, we have mis-
used the Divine urge. If we use the urge to perform a service that is beneficial to ourselves and others, that is a
constructive use. Robbing is born out of fear of not

having enough and choosing to take from others. Love is giving of ourselves, our talents and resources to help humankind and this planet."

(Love is generous)

Drummond says, "We have truth in Nature as it comes from God. And it has to be read with the same unbiased mind. The same open eye, the same faith. The same reverence as all other revelations." Intangible Love can only be made tangible through us. Ernest Holmes, in his *Science of Mind* textbook, says: "Any scientist who refuses to accept intangible values has no adequate basis for the values which he has already discovered. . . . We do well to listen to this Inner Voice, for it tells us of a life wonderful in its scope; of a Love beyond our fondest dreams; of a freedom which the soul craves."

The principle of Love may be hidden from our external sight. An inward gaze, provoked by intuition, generates the external feelings that we all recognize as love.

Spirit as Love and Law

Spirit as Love is the energy source that is all-pervasive. It is constantly giving of Itself. It is the life force Itself. *Spirit as Law* is the subjective mind that operates on our emotion-based thoughts. Thoughts are things. Our thoughts are colored by our beliefs and amplified by our feelings. Psychosomatic science is producing much evidence of the mind/body relationship. This relationship is covered well in the book I've written called *Licking Your Wounds*.

The Law of God is impersonal. It gives us free choice to rob a bank or to build one. By our deeds we are known. What we put in comes out. The Law is no respecter of person, place or thing. It is exact. As scientists, we discover and use the Law to bring about the results we desire. Like the law of electricity, we discover and use it. If we use it with Love, we are fulfilling the Law.

Within Love and Law is intelligence. The will-to-good governs. Eleanor Roosevelt said, "It is better to light a candle than to curse the dark." She was an intelligent lady who understood how the Law works. Jesus understood the Law when he said, "Of myself I do nothing, it is the Father within that does the work." Jesus fulfilled the Law by expressing Love completely. Love is Light. We need to bring light from our heart to our mind, and dismiss dark thoughts. According to the Law, we cannot escape the consequences of our choices. The only redemption is Love, and something in us knows that. Call that "something" the Father within, the Holy Comforter, intuition or revelation—it makes no difference, even if we fail to recognize It. Failing to recognize It does not mean It does not exist. As Joseph Campbell put it, "Follow your Bliss."

To Illustrate

Please note: Love and Law are inseparable and appear to be interchangeable. We can't have one without the other. They are like the particle/wave in the study of physics. You can describe them separately, but under close observation, one becomes the other, and they cannot be separated.

To illustrate how Love and Law work, please view the cross appearing below. Notice that the vertical lines and horizontal lines are equal and open. They are open, because there is no end to Love and Law. Law is on the horizontal plane. Love is on the vertical plane. The place where they converge is the Christ fulfillment of the Law.

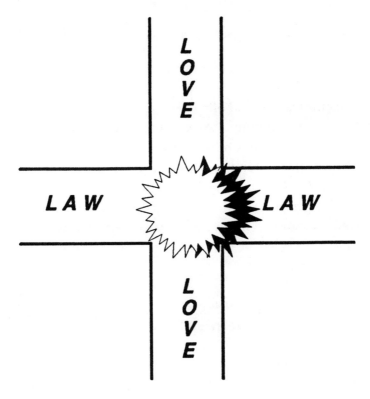

How Love and Law Work

The bright sun represents love fulfilling the Law of being—the Christ-like individual, the Love Pilgrim, dynamically living Love. The dark shadow represents horizontal thinking: Law without Love's fullness is only a shadow of what is real.

Love comes in on the vertical plane as inspiration, intuition. It is using our infundibulum, the Divine input. The law must act on and produce like kind. That is why it is essential that we understand the nature of thought. The disease of "touchiness" is insensitive to love and ignores the vertical, divine thoughts.

Horizontal Thinking

It seems humankind often gets stuck on the treadmill of horizontal thinking. "An eye for an eye, a tooth for a tooth" perpetuates more of the same. "So most of the world walks around blind and toothless," as someone says in *Fiddler on the Roof*. There is no immunity from the consequences of taking revenge. What goes around, comes around. The law of cause and effect is a just and exact law. What we put into the creative medium reflects back on us.

Vertical Thinking

Undistorted vertical thinking brings Love into all of our thoughts, deeds and activities. It is through God's grace that we have awakened to this understanding. Jesus, the Master Teacher and wonderful example, showed us the way. The Christ, the Light of God in all of us, is a soul quality, a divine pattern, Love's essence, the Father within.

The divine input of Love gets distorted by fear. We often hold grievances that seem to distort the purity of the input. We may hold a belief in lack and limitation, resulting in an insufficient supply of funds. We may not have enough self-esteem to deliver our talents for an adequate income.

Love is the greatest gift. But it is not a possession to be saved. To appreciate It, It must be spent in the coin of the realm, in the Spirit as intended. Everyone has it, but few of us have spent it to its maximum human potential. "Love alone is capable of uniting living beings in such a way as to complete and fulfill them, for it alone takes them and joins them by what is deepest in themselves," says Pierre Teilhard de Chardin.

Grievances Mean Living in the Past

Holding a grievance against our brother indicates we are living in the past. When we hold grievances, we are misusing the vitality in the moment. We all do it. But God will help us change if we want to change.

Today, it is very popular to blame the way we are on our upbringing. We find fault with our parents or with our lack of them. It is true. Some of us spend a whole lifetime playing a cassette tape of "poor me." That is horizontal thinking without Love. We will always be able to learn from the mistakes of our parents, but only if we want to learn.

Middle-Aged Businessman

Recentlly in Dublin, Ireland, a middle-aged business-man, whom we will call Ken, confided in me. He and his brother grew up in the same family, yet they were as different as day and night. Ken was an optimist and his brother a pessimist. When Ken visited his brother in Belfast, his sibling was "up in arms." His brother would have a few drinks and voice his rage at the people in a small neighboring community. Ken asked his brother, "What is disturbing you?" The brother said, "They have killed 250 people in that small neighboring town." Ken said, "I did not read anything about it in the Dublin newspaper. When did it happen?" His brother replied, "Three hundred and fifty years ago." He had learned of the event from his parents, and they from their parents, etc.

Ken's brother is preoccupied with rage, dwelling on evil. His "bloody" mind is producing more of the same. He is repeating the same mistakes of his parents, and that of some of his ancestors. What we give our attention to determines our attitude. On the othcr end of the spectrum from his brother, Ken was an optimist. He was using his creative talents to produce sales of products beneficial to society's needs. It was most pleasant sharing ideas with good-tempered Ken.

Grievances or prejudices are always a thing of the past. It takes Love in the present moment to let them go. Sincere forgiveness opens the vertical portal of Love awareness.

(Love thinks no evil, and hopeth all good things)

The means of accessing awareness of God is "to keep the high watch," being vertically attuned to seeking Love's essence in every moment, in every way. This is a simple concept built on a wonderful principle.

(Living Love is the answer.)

Please note, in the illustration on page 69, at the intersection of the cross, where Love is expressed into Law, we have answered the clarion call as an expression of Love. There we are fulfilling the Law of our being. We cast no shadows. Our Love is the light we cast through inspired living. All inspirational living comes through the Holy Comforter where the will of God is known. As we intentionally align our thoughts to think on that which is vertically attuned, we become pure of heart.

Drummond understood that. "We must become so pure in heart—and it needs much practice—that we shall see God." If we can understand how the law works and that spaceship earth is our classroom, we can understand a lot of suffering. "God put man in the crucible and makes him pure by fire," explains Life. . . . "To me to live in Christ" is the answer, according to Drummond. Christ is the soul quality that fulfills the Law as Love.

Thoughts Uttered through Things

Drummond felt that the external or temporal had value. "The temporal is the husk and framework of the eternal. *Thoughts can only be uttered through things.* The temporal is but the scaffolding of the eternal. When the last immaterial souls have climbed through this material to God, the scaffolding shall be taken down. The earth dissolved with fervent heat, not because it is evil, but because its work is done."

Thoughts as Things

The paradox is that Life's challenges always show up in the husk, the outer form, from skin rash to cancer, from poverty to environmental disturbances to relationships. The solution is always the same. It lies in VERTICAL THINKING, the eternal thoughts that make up the full spectrum of Love. Love is our divine passion. Compassion is how we spend it. Unkind thoughts, egotistical thoughts, fearful thoughts are horizontal and need to be dismissed quickly in favor of vertical thoughts. Thoughts show up as things, like shadows. Love is the only thing that is real. Thoughts of Divine Love cast no shadow.

Love is Light. Drummond would command his classes "to look at the things which are not seen." He invites us to look at the temporal but not to pause. "You must penetrate it. Go through it, and see its shadow, its spiritual shadow, on the further side. For truly, the first thing seen is the shadow, the thing on the other side the reality. The sap to make the budding Christ come out is from God, from the indwelling immanent Christ."

Phenomena of the Spiritual World

Drummond appreciated the deep thinkers who penetrated the outer world to the vastness of inner truth. Few have dared to seek the meaning of the infinite in the finite, the eternal in the temporal. Yet everyone who expresses Love does it. Beauty is Love's fragrance. Peace, joy and intelligence are its vibration and tone. Truth is its celebration. Heaven is its reward.

There is a guidance system within us, a will to good that can take us home. Many persons on the planet today are discovering that the Spirit within is beckoning us to love. As we Love God, ourselves and each other, our intuitive faculty quickens. We begin to realize we are part of a greater whole. We are each awakening to God's will and recognizing Its presence. A dear friend and poet put it this way.

My Shepherd

I feel the hand of God on me
    like a friend to whom I'm known,
Leading me down better roads
    than I would take alone.
His guidance helps me through the days
    when I need His help to cope,
And at night, He gives me peace and rest
    and soothes my heart with hope.

I feel the Love of Christ in me,
    the Love He said I'd know
If I'd just put my trust in Him
    and let my hatreds go.
And so I'll hate no man again
    the way I've done before.
Instead, I do the best I can
    to "Go and sin no more."

The hand of God, the Love of Christ
    are in my daily life,
And now I live in Love and peace
    where once I dwelt in strife.
My life is richer now by far
    than anything before,
For my Shepherd leads me in His steps
    on the path to Heaven's door.

                                        Bill Hazel

Intuition and Intellect

One of the intellectual giants of the twentieth century is
Ernest Holmes. He synthesized religion, philosophy,
science and poetry. Holmes had this to say in *Ideas of
Power* (p. 140): "The intellect may analyze, dissect, accept, or reject; but there is an intuitional faculty back of
the intellect that knows more than the intellect. We do
not all grab it right up like that. Therefore we have to
train the intellect to reach a place where it receives this
greater illumination. And that is what I mean by stretch-
ing the mind."

In 1901, a Canadian psychiatrist, Dr. Richard M.
Bucke, author of the book *Cosmic Consciousness*, described
the intuitive mind. "We have the intuitional mind . . .
the mind whose highest element is not a recept [recep-
tacle] or a concept [notion] but an intuition. This is the
mind in which sensation, simple consciousness and self
consciousness are supplemented and crowned with cosmic consciousness." Gautama the Buddha, Jesus the
Christ, Paul the Apostle, Mohammed, William Blake,
Walt Whitman and many more are described in his
book. Dr. Bucke and Ernest Holmes both had illuminating experiences in their lives.

The Way to Love

The point is: we all have an intellect and an intuitive
faculty. It takes intellectual discipline to develop the more

important use of the intuition. Horizontal thinking is not enough. Vertical alignment to the intuitive process is necessary for the involution of Spirit. In order for Spirit to flow in more freely, Spirit must be consciously sought after and realized. Make no mistake, God is everywhere present. God is in us, around us and throughout all creation. If God is Love and we want more Love in our lives, the answer is simple! First we must understand what Love is and what it is not. Secondly, we must express it. Thirdly, it is in the giving of Love that we receive it. We can only give Love if we have it, if we live it, if we be it.

What Is Your Outward Sign?

What is your outward sign? What is my outward sign? Our bodies are an outward sign of an inner conviction. Broken hearts, emotionally or physically, are often the result of not understanding and expressing true Love. Arthritis is often a sign of rigid thinking over a prolonged period of time. The stones we cast at others as ministers, parents, bosses, or gossips usually come back to hit us . . . if not in this life, in the next. That is why St. Paul says, ''Love beareth all things.''

If we don't believe in the continuity of life, we might be right. Or we may be denying the intuitive faculty, a faculty that is greater than we are and yet is available to all of us. There have been great intellects and great intuitives. Intellect without intuition is like Law without Love.

One time I went to a doctor who was able to help me in an emergency. He mechanically relieved the urine from my bladder. I have been assisted more than once by people in the medical profession who have learned to use the tools of their trade with much skill, caring and concern. That is Love. People in any profession, however, can become very materialistic and can be ruled by fear rather than Love. All of us can become so caught up in our self-importance that our intellect closes the portal to divine guidance. Gifts that come through our intuition are blocked by our self-importance. Note the example that follows, called "Warning Signs."

Warning Signs

At another time, a doctor told me that I needed to have exploratory surgery for my prostate. The procedure would require me to stay a few days, or more, in the hospital. He showed me a well-prepared brochure on the subject, with colored pictures. He was using all his skills to sell me on this operation. I asked him, "How much time do I have to decide?" He replied, "A week." I said, "Could I take two weeks or a month? I believe in the power of prayer." He replied, "I believe in the power of prayer too. But if you let this go, you will be *begging* for my services in six months."

(Love does not puff up onself)

Insistence and intellectual pride are two red flags in my book. I never went back to him. Prayer was my answer. Affirmative prayer.

Sometime later, when I was on an airplane, I engaged in conversation with a young man who was on his way to a urologists' convention. He informed me, ''There are many prostate operations being performed unnecessarily.'' My intuition lighted up and confirmed that the choice I had made was correct. There is an Infinite Mind that knows all and sees all.

A few years later, I had the prostate checked again by a doctor I felt I could trust. In his office he performed a simple, low-cost surgical procedure. All was well, thank God. Love had guided me—through intuition—in making the right choice.

Law of Attraction

Where our interests are, so are we. ''Birds of a feather flock together.'' Activity follows interest, form follows thought like night follows day. You are interested in Love, so you read this book, as I have read many others on the subject. None of us has the ''only'' answer. Each of us has as much right to Love as anyone else, and we are evolving in our understanding of Love. The evolutionary development of Love in ourselves depends on how much we can embody Love in our thoughts, deeds and activities.

Embodying Love

To embody Love means to fill our life with it by choice, to do consciously what It would have us do. Love is greater than we are, yet we have access to it through our intuitive faculty.

The poem appearing several pages back came from Love. Infinite Love as intelligence, creative life force, God-the-Father-within is the Source. Ernest Holmes called it "The Thing Itself." The wonder of it is, It uses us to the extent of our receptivity to It. "The intellect identifies itself with the Spirit until it makes possible a greater influx of Spirit into the intellect," says Holmes.

I have read about, and met, an ever-increasing number of people who are finding the courage to acknowledge and follow their internal guidance system. Courage is involved, because we are often required to reevaluate our old beliefs and patterns and dismantle the ones that no longer serve the greater good. The greater theology, the greater science, the greater idea is often met with resistance from people who are not ready to change.

There is no idea, there is no power, there is no presence greater than Love. Love is the seed of our being, just as the acorn is the seed of the oak tree. To know Love and to serve its source is to identify with truth. Intuition is the name; accessing it is the game.

PART IV

Love: How to Cooperate with It

We have looked at: "Love: How to Recognize It"; "Love: How It Works"; and "Love: What It Does." And now we come to "Love: How to Cooperate With It." In other words, how we cooperate with God as Love and God as Law. To better understand how God works through us requires some investigation on our part. Understanding the relationship between Spirit, mind and matter is helpful in learning to cooperate with God.

How Spirit Works

Spirit is the origin of words and thoughts. Spirit expresses the Divine word in Universal Mind. As an example, say the word Love originates first in the mind of the Father God. Spirit is like the Father God, and Mind is like the Mother God. The Mother God takes the word given to her by the Father and nurtures the word in her womb. The birth of the conceived and nurtured word is called the Son. The illumined Christ is the Divine word (Love) expressed. The word Love is a Divine idea, placed in

Universal Mind. Universal Mind acts as a medium. Universal Mind has no choice; It must act upon the thought given. It is the Law in action. The birth of the word is the materialization. It is made whole or holy. The form Love has taken at any particular moment depends on Its use in the Law.

Plato, Plotinus, Swedenborg, Bacon, Pascal, and Emerson were no strangers to Professor Drummond. What they all had in common was a good grasp of how Spirit, mind and form were One. Carlyle said, "All visible things are emblems. What thou seest is not there on its own account; strictly speaking [it] is not there at all. Matter exists only spiritually, and to represent some idea and body it forth." In order words, ideas become forms. The form is a symbol of what we have in our own mind.

How Thoughts Take Form

I like to use the analogy of a personal computer to demonstrate how the Law of Mind works through us. God can be represented as the Universal Computer where all enlightened, intelligent ideas are stored. Our own mind is an individualization of Divine Mind. We all have modems that can access Divine Mind. This access is called intuition. Divine Mind (Mother God) is programmed by Spirit (Father God) to express Love, Joy, Peace. The enlightened child accesses Divine Mind through the intuitive faculty and brings the divine pattern of thoughts through. The inspired thoughts register in our subconscious mind, which is like a personal computer. As we access the thoughts in our subconsicous mind, they become conscious. The conscious thoughts then show up on our monitor, or screen. They now become our experience. Spirit has taken form as our experience. That is how Spirit works.

How Subconscious Mind Works

What shows up on our screen is colored by our beliefs and our perception. Our subconscious mind, or our personal computer, may be filled with mega bytes, or stored thoughts, that fall short of our divine potential. The keyboard, or word-processing keys, represent the choices that we have to input. This concept is most important. We can decide what to store in memory and when to access it. What we give our attention to shows up eventually in our experience. That is my understanding of how the Law of Mind works. What we put into mind must show up eventually as our experience. We cannot change the Law of our being.

We can *cooperate with what God is. And what God is, is Love.* There is a way to invite Love into our every thought. This is covered in the section called *"infundibulum."* Infundibulum is our modem for accessing Universal Spirit.

Professor Drummond put it in this way: "The discovery of Law is simply the discovery of Science." As a teacher of science, philosophy and religion, he declared

it brilliantly this way: "*THOUGHTS CAN BE UT-
TERED ONLY THROUGH THINGS.* THE POSI-
TION WE HAVE BEEN LED TO TAKE IS NOT
THAT THE SPIRITUAL LAWS ARE ANALO-
GOUS TO THE NATURAL LAWS, BUT THAT
THEY ARE THE SAME LAWS." Now get this: "*IT
IS NOT A QUESTION OF ANALOGY BUT ONE OF
IDENTITY.*" To my understanding, he is saying that at
one end we are dealing with matter and at the other end
with Spirit. But we can change what appears on our per-
sonal screen by changing our way of thinking.

There was no doubt in Drummond's mind that the
greatest teacher of all times was Jesus. Why? Because
Jesus the man identified with God. How did he do it? He
said, "Of myself I can do nothing, it is the Father within
that does the work." Jesus knew God to be Love. Love
is no less in Emerson, Gandhi, Martin Luther King or
in us. If Love has not surfaced in our lives very much,
it would follow that we have not identified with it. In
other words, we don't know God.

Henry used the word *Life* as a synonym for Love, as
Jesus often did. "Life is definite and resident. Spiritual
life is not a visit from a force, but a resident tenant in the
soul."

The Supreme Principle

Henry Drummond understood that God is love and that
Love is the fulfillment of Natural Law, prompting him

to say, "The supreme principle upon which we have to run our lives is to adhere, through good report and ill will, through temptation and prosperity and adversity, to the will of God. Wherever that will may lead us. . . . There is no happiness or success in any life till that principle is taken possession of." Because God is Love, and we are made in God's image and likeness. If we are not expressing true Love, we will never know who we are, or what God is. If we do not identify with God as Love, we suffer from an identity crisis.

God's Will

Drummond believed that it is the will of God for us to be happy. He would say, "Do not sacrifice to a thing that is disagreeable unless you are quite sure it is God's will. God's will does not always lie in the line of the disagreeable. My meat and my drink, Christ said, 'is to do the will of Him that sent me.' " How do we know if we are responding to God's will? What is it like? The answer is to use your *infundibulum*.

Infundibulum

A special friend and a spiritual teacher, Archbishop Warren P. Watters, at the age of 101 introduced me and my wife Bobbe to this word, *infundibulum*. Bobbe was in the process of revising the popular book written in the 1960s by Maxwell Maltz, *Psycho-Cybernetics*. Bishop Watters had known numerous spiritual and psychological teachers personally in his many decades of teaching. I felt it important that Bobbe meet with him at his home in Santa Barbara, California.

He gave us this word *infundibulum* as a gift, in response to her question, "I know this is very simplistic and naive, but how do you think I can best impart to my reader how to achieve the happiness habit?"

He smiled and took her hand. "My dear, lovely woman, let me give you a word. Words are precious gifts. The word is *infundibulum*."

Bobbe and I had no clue to its meaning. With a twinkle in his eye he challenged us to look it up in one of the many dictionaries on his library shelves. We read the definition out loud.

INFUNDIBULUM: 1. The hollow conical process of gray matter to which the pituitary body is continuous with the brain.   2. Funnel.

Secret of Happiness

Bobbe asked him to elaborate on the word *funnel*. "Funnel is the secret of happiness. Yes, that is it," he said smiling, happily playing with us. "Every day I meditate on happiness. I see the great Universal funneling through the top of my head and through my being. Here in my mental-emotional-spiritual infundibulum, I let it all pass through me. *I accept everyone and everything as being in its right and proper place.* My infundibulum allows me to funnel the spiritual into the material until they blend into one. When it's working, I am able to think with my heart and hear with my head.''

For many years Archbishop Watters published the periodical *Esoteric Review.* He knew esoteric meant "hidden" to some, but "revelation" to others. His work is being carried on today by a church he founded called The Free Church of Antioch. Although it is one of many independent, Christian, Catholic and Episcopal sacramental churches, it technically has at least twelve lines of Apostolic succession. The church can trace its succession to the church at Antioch founded in A.D. 38 by St. Peter. Antioch is the place where the new cult first called itself Christian.

Funnel Consciousness

So what does this mean as far as guidance is concerned? If God is Love, then we each need to seek the resemblance of Love in our prayer and meditations. We need to funnel the awareness of Love. We need to embody Love. We need to be Love. Where do we find Love? "In the secret place of the Most High.''

An Example of Funnel Consciousness

As I wrote this section in York, England, I happened upon a young white man I'll call Ron. Ron was entertaining the tourists in a shopping mall. He was playing a strange instrument known as a digeriedigeriedo. (I am not sure how to spell it.) It is a wind instrument developed and played by the oldest group of people found on this planet, the Aborigines of Australia. Members of this oldest living culture of people on our planet today were mistreated by the invading forces which imposed their ways on the natives. The Aborigines were removed from their homelands and forced to live under foreign rule. Because of this, the white man was viewed with suspicion. The Aborigines were not interested any more in teaching the offensive white man their ways.

I asked the young man Ron how he was able to learn to use this most difficult wind instrument. "Did they, the Aborigines, teach you?" "Not exactly," he said. "Did they show or tell you?" I persisted. "No. It was more of a spiritual experience. I believe there is only one Spirit. I learned with my heart at a soul level. It did take me a few years living near them to become proficient at it. Spirit gave them the idea to build this instrument and to imitate the sounds of native animals. The same Spirit gave me the talents to do the same."

God gives to them that seek. This is the Law of Attraction. What we give our attention to, what we put our conscious mind to, eventually shows up as our experience.

This young man has a well-developed infundibulum. A funnel consciousness allows him to relate at the soul level, where we are all one in Spirit, one with infinite Intelligence, one with Love, one with the Law of our being. The creative genius in us all never ceases to amaze me. Some are more proficient than others at accessing It. But the portal is open to all who seek, knock and ask. Is it not? As Archbishop Watters put it, "We think with our heart and listen with our head." Jesus said, "I go unto the Father." The Father within can only be discerned spiritually. Love is the portal through which funnel conciousness works.

Love Eased Her Pain

A great lesson for me occurred when my mother-in-law, Eddythe, was making her transition from the physical world. She had been diagnosed with pancreatic cancer, and the doctor gave her six months to live. She did all she knew to lick the disease, not from a sense of fear but for the joy of living. As she got weaker and more jaundiced, her close friends would visit her and cry. Their crying disturbed her more than the illness. She learned to live in the moment and to appreciate the now. She was not obscured by the past or by projecting into the future. *The omni-present is where Love abides.*

(Love endureth all things)

Eddythe died to the physical in six months as medical science had predicted. They also predicted intense pain, suffering and hospitalization, with drugs to relieve the pain. But that did not happen. I spent the last night with her in her home. As the life force was leaving her body and there was discomfort with the physical deterioration, she would call out with a whisper of a voice, "Charles, would you please dampen my dry gums?" And with all the strength that she could muster, she whispered in my ear, "Charles, I love you." Her spiritual strength was most impressive. Her funnel to the Divine was open, accessed and expressed.

(Love beareth all things)

Thoughts Eternal

Peace that goes beyond the comprehension of a fearful mind is an attribute of Love. Disease is always in the temporal. Fear is always in the temporal. Love, however, is the essence and character of the eternal. Too often we become hypnotized by *things* . . . such as colds, terminal illness or self-importance and miss the eternal truth in the precious moment. Love is the only emancipator and fear its only adversary. It takes our cooperation to open the funnel to Love's consciousness. Only Love can render fear powerless. To attain peace, we must desire to access and to express Love. We must develop our infundibulum. It is our modem or access to the Divine Principle stored in the memory of the Eternal. God thoughts are eternal. Our thoughts are temporal unless they equal the Divine attributes of Love. That is what St. Paul, Professor Drummond and I are endeavoring to sort out for ourselves and the reader . . . a frame of reference of what Love is and what it is not.

Some Thoughts Are Temporal

Our thoughts are temporal if they do not resemble Love. On the other hand, our thoughts are more than things when they express the Divine attributes of Love. We can recognize these attributes in the Prayer of St. Francis of Assisi. As we learn to open our infundibulum, we become instruments of the Almighty. If we sow temporal-type thoughts, such as injury, doubt, despair, darkness, sadness, hate and fear, the Law will oblige us and produce these temporary conditions in our experience.

If we sow Love, pardon, faith, hope, light and joy, we give expression to the eternal. Then we are a beneficial presence. We are awakening to our true nature, Love. St. Francis understood what God wants and how the Law works. He called the Father within, *Divine Master.* "O Divine Master, grant that I may not so much seek to be consoled as to console; to be understood as to understand; to be loved as to love. For it is in giving that we receive. It is in pardoning that we are pardoned. It is in dying that we are born to eternal life."

Love Is the Emancipator

Henry Drummond, toward the end of his physical life, had a chronic affliction of the bones. Probably today we would call it cancer. Whatever it was, it maimed him greatly. He was confined to lying on his back for more than a year. A memorial sketch by John Watson said this: "It seemed as if his sufferings liberated and revealed the forces of his soul. . . . Those who saw him in his illness saw that, as the physical life flickered low, the spiritual energy grew. Always gentle and considerate, he became even more careful, more tender, more thoughtful, more unselfish. He never in any way complained." Only fear thinks it has something to lose and distorts the channel of Truth.

(Love suffereth long and is patient)

Watson recalled what Drummond said of a friend's death: "Putting by the well-worn tools without a sigh, and expecting elsewhere better work to do." Drummond felt that there was something better than pleasure or pain in the world—and that something is progress. The result of progress is evolution. The cause and momentum of progress is involution. That which is channeled purely through the infundibulum is Love. That which seems to distort Love during our journey is fear.

(Love hopeth all things)

The Hunchback

I was introduced to a hunchbacked woman who had been coming to Dennis Fare, a well-known healing therapist, for fifteen years for treatment. Her mother shared with me this information that I now paraphrase: "My daughter was born a hunchback. For fifteen years we tried everything medically possible. Nothing worked. She was hopelessly bent in two like a nutcracker. She could not stand erect. Our funds had run low, and a friend suggested we go to Dennis, who makes no charge for his work. As you can see, we are not sorry we went for spiritual healing. My daughter is no longer bent over and has made slow and steady progress.''

(Love is generous and patient)

While Dennis and one of his students did contact healing, he explained what he was doing by way of gentle massage and manipulation. He felt that soon the complete healing might take place and explained why. ''The collapsed back has progressed to a place where, with a slight change, the vertebrae can straighten out gradually.''

(Love has hope)

The daughter was now 30. The mother, daughter and therapist are well pleased at the 15-year progress. Happiness is an attribute of Love. Hope keeps the vertical channel to funnel consciousness open. Fear of making no progress will keep the channel to greater love awareness closed.

Blessed Assurance

Dennis is well aware that it is God that heals. God is the only power. There is no force in opposition to God.

There is only misuse of God's power, stemming from our ignorance. All of the world's challenges are but a call to Love. The only sin is ignorance of what God wants. God is Love. The only redemption comes through Love. Love restores our awareness of what we are, children of God. As Dennis is expressing Love in his work, his intuitive faculty is wide open. He often feels or becomes more aware of Love's presence. This feeling that we are all One in God provides Dennis and his clients with a sense of assurance.

We can know with blessed assurance that we are part of something greater than ourselves, and yet, at the same time we are an individualization of It. This blessed assurance brings a knowingness that Love is holy, that expressing Love is the ''whole'' business, that identifying with the Father within is not optional. We are trusting in something that is greater than we are, yet we are in It. Within God is Love, Intelligence, Law, Abundance and Blessed Assurance. The answers are within us, for we are within God. When we give ourselves over to fear and frustration, we are identifying with a consciousness of poverty, lack and limitation. Expressing Love offers the only lasting assurance because God is Love, and God as Love lasts forever.

Love Vaunteth Not Itself

Sometimes my patience runs out. I think something has to happen according to my will, to my schedule, to my time frame, to my scheme, to my goals. As a healing facilitator, I forget sometimes and fall into horizontal thinking. I want everyone that I pray for to get better. I think I am the fixer. If there is no sign of progress, meaning that the physical healing is not evident, I can get frustrated. My frustration is evidence that I am placing my trust in something smaller than "I AM." My personal computer seems powerless. Under my frustration is a fear of not looking good. Making myself important and powerful is a seducing glamor that leads to a fall.

Enlightened Work

The more enlightened work I do requires getting my "bloated nothingness" out of the way. I need to give up the things that I can't alter and turn to Love. Love brings peace and assurance to any moment. As I love, the fear and frustration dissolve to the nothingness from whence they came. In the "holy instant" that Love is recognized, things change for the better. My frustrations, I now know, are an invitation to vertical thinking. My horizontal thinking is troublesome. In it, I am unaware of what God wants. My vertical thinking accesses Love and takes me out of self-importance. I am still an awakening student of what I understand God wants.

Opening the Love Portal

Sometimes, being of service to others in a way that feels good opens the vertical portal to Love's channel. Sometimes affirmative prayer, meditation, good music or the gentle caring Love of a friend or animal activates Love's awareness. Sometimes pain and suffering are also invitations to Love's call. This subject is well covered in my book called *Licking Your Wounds*. The greatest gift available to us in cooperating with what God wants is the act of forgiveness. "Without forgiveness life is governed by . . . an endless cycle of resentment and retaliation," writes Roberto Assagioli. *No one can know true Love who holds a grievance against anyone.* "Love worketh no ill to his neighbor: therefore Love is the fulfilling of the Law" (Romans 8:10).

Our Essential Nature

If we understand that God is Love and that we are children of God, we too must be of the same Essence. Our essential nature is Love. Drummond, St. Paul and others are saying we must recognize our inward nature and claim it. Draw it through us. As we focus inwardly, we choose Love to bring forth into our inevitable experience. "Rest and Peace [and Love] are but claims in man's *inward nature*, and arise through causes as definite and inevitable," says Drummond.

Love as a Miracle

"Miracles can occur anywhere. When someone cares, when years of animosity and resentment disappear in one act of compassion, when indifference is wiped away by an outstretched hand offered to help, when a human life is changed by one simple act of Love . . . these are indeed miracles''—this from Leo Buscaglia's latest book, *Born for Love.* All life resembles a miracle as we awaken to Love's call.

Inner Guidance in a "Terminal" Situation

One event that I was privileged to be a part of stands out fresh in my mind as if it happened yesterday. Seven years ago, my wife received a telephone call. A friend of hers, whom I knew only casually, was in the intensive care ward of a local hospital. When we went to visit her, my wife did not recognize Joan (a fictitious name). We looked through an internal window and could see Joan was swollen up like a balloon. The head nurse only allowed us to look through the window for one minute.

Driving away from the hospital, I got a strong urge to go back. A tingling sensation, accompanied with some thoughts of doing prayer work with Joan for "ten minutes," was paramount in my mind. I felt these good thoughts needed to be acted out. I told my wife about my desire to go back to the hospital. "I want to ask the nurse if I can have 'ten minutes' of quality time alone with Joan." My wife understood and asked me to drop her off at her appointment.

I entered the intensive care section of the hospital and explained that I was a minister, here to see Joan. I was ushered into a preparatory room where I was instructed to put on a white gown and plastic gloves. Joan was on the cusp of leaving this world. Her liver had accidentally been cut into and was polluting her body, and she was lying on her back with numerous life-support systems monitoring, feeding and medicating her body. She was conscious and trying to tell me something through her oxygen mask, but I could not understand her. After several failed attempts, I asked the head nurse if she could understand her. The nurse listened, and Joan asked for "ten minutes" of time alone with me. My intuitions flashed and caught a glimpse of the guidance system that had brought us together.

The nurse adjusted the various equipment to allow Joan and me some private quiet time together. I told Joan I would pray for her. I knew I must not focus on the problem and the drama surrounding this situation. God is the only healer, and Christ, the enlightened within each of us, cannot be destroyed. I anointed the center of Joan's forehead with my right hand as I held her left hand in my left hand. "In the name of the Father and of the Son and of the Living Spirit, we are One," I prayed. As I continued to pray, the power of Love flowed powerfully through me into and around us. Joan's body twitched all over as if a strong current were passing through it.

After about one minute passed in prayer, I never had felt such a strong life force before. I could feel that Joan's body was relieved of tension. A sense of peace filled my awareness as I decided to spend the remaining nine minutes in prayer thanking God for bringing us together and using us for Its channel. As I took the plastic gloves off,

I noticed the lines in my hands seemed to have left brown imprints on the clear plastic. I held the gloves up to show Joan. "Look, the heat from my hands seems to have left burn marks that resemble the creases in my hands."

A week later Joan was out of the hospital and convalescing at home. I later found out she had a near-death experience prior to my arrival on the scene, at which time Joan's signs of life in this world diminished to almost none. The head nurse was very instrumental in calling her back to a this-world awareness. Something in the nurse prompted her to keep calling Joan's spirit back into her body for three hours. Something in Joan knew her spirit was to return to her body. Out of her body, she was shown the hidden splendor beyond the corporal . . . a hidden splendor more beautiful than words can adequately describe. My words, too, seem to me inadequate to describe Love and Its guidance system. So I hope you will read them with your heart.

Prescription for Happiness

In our American culture we offer assurance to someone we're assisting by saying "no problem." In Great Britain, they say "not to worry." We offer assurance because we know fear is a problem. It is not the devil that is doing it to us. The worries are manufactured by our way of thinking. We often make the mistake of putting our trust in something other than Love. We don't like to take responsibility for the way we think. We play helpless and say, "I can't change the way I think." Or we place blame on ourselves or others for our unhappiness. These attitudes are not Love.

There is something in us that looks for security in the material world or in relationships. Real security can't be found there. Deep within the substance of matter and relationships lies Love. To investigate and discover real happiness starts with the way we think. To change the way we think requires interest and work. We Love Pilgrims have reached the point of commitment to making the effort.

St. Paul gave a wonderful prescription to the Philippians who were worried and unhappy. "Whatever is true, whatever is noble, whatever is right, whatever is pure, whatever is lovely, whatever is admirable. . . . If anything is excellent or praiseworthy. . . . THINK ABOUT SUCH THINGS." Wow! That is more than positive thinking, it is affirmative thinking. We are identifying with and in agreement with profound truth. This is the "Golden Key" of Emmet Fox, whose method of praying has helped many. This is the foundation of Spiritual Mind Science. This is the foundation of all healing work demonstrated by Jesus the Christ.

Love Is Not Easy

No one ever said that Love was easy. But in the last analysis, it is not the problems that Love brings to us, but rather what we bring to Love that really matters. . . .

The conflicts we encounter in loving are often simply opportunities which ask for a little extra effort on our part.
Perhaps we need to see innocence in another's transgressions, and not be so critical of them. Perhaps we need to
be silent and listen more often with our hearts. We may
find it better making allowance than making points.
Perhaps we'd be wiser to overlook weaknesses rather than
playing on them.

Leo Buscaglia, thanks for your words of wisdom.

The Greatest Importer and Exporter

There is no book, philosophy, science or religion that can
contain or limit Love. The human form is not a con-
tainer, it is a channel. It is a funnel that imports and ex-
ports Love. The greatest importer and exporter of Love
known to humankind is Jesus the Christ. Jesus knew that
He was a channel for God the Father; and God the
Mother, the Holy Comforter, God as Spirit, God as
Love, is what the Christ is. The Christ is in God, and we
are in the Christ. True Love cannot be contained in any
one form. But it can be realized. Love is everywhere present. It is praiseworthy, excellent and beautiful.

Ignorance Is No Excuse

There is no end to Love, inspiration or guidance. We are
not unworthy of God's Love, inspiration or guidance; we

are simply ignorant. Ignorance is derived from the root word "ignore." We ignore Love's impulses to do or say the correct thing. We ignore the warning signs of our transgressions or those of others. The root of all transgressions is fear, not Love. We Love Pilgrims are learning to choose Love instead of fear. We cannot adequately define Love, but something in us responds to Love and understands Its impulse. As we follow the potential of Love, we begin to have a clearer idea of what Love is and what Love is not.

The prophets of old warned us to live the "Golden Rule." God was giving us guidance from without through a series of messengers called prophets. Messages came via angels, burning bushes, floods, stars, dreams, voices, etc. Perhaps we were too dense in body and mind to get the message in any other way. About two thousand years ago, humankind was introduced to a new level of understanding . . . that we are spiritual beings expressing through a dense body form. It was time for us to begin learning that guidance, the presence of God, is not just in the *external* but also in the *internal*. Jesus and many of his disciples discovered that this internal awareness grew through the expression of Love, not lip service to the shallow words that say "I love you" but rather a conscious dedication to live It. To know God is to express Love. To see God is perhaps impossible, but to *know* is possible to the Love Pilgrim.

God Is Love and Law

God is both Love and Law, an invisible Presence and an invisible Principle. The Presence is Love, and although we cannot see it, we can sense it. Light is a good metaphor for Love. It is very common to see light. What is not so common is to see the light rays. Without the invisible light rays there would be no light, and without God there would be no Love. This morning while I was taking a shower, the sunlight was reflecting off a mirror and coming through the clear glass door to the shower stall. The fine mist in the shower provided a substance that clearly showed rays of light. Dust particles will sometimes do the same thing. The particles give definition to the otherwise invisible rays. We ourselves are similar to the mist and the dust particles. As we choose to express Love, those normally invisible Love rays become apparent in our activities. We might say "We bring Love to Light in the mist (midst) of what we do."

Christos

The Christos, the God light rays, are invisible waves that make themselves visible by means of using particles. The particles reveal the otherwise invisible presence of the wave. The materialist identifies with the particle. The Christ-like person identifies with the invisible wave. The wave, metaphorically, is the omnipresent Spirit. It is what is excellent, praiseworthy, intelligent, beautiful and true. That is the wavelength that is a constant broadcast of Love. We call this constant holy wave the Christos, the Spirit of the Divine in humankind.

Through our ignorance, we often have interrupted the broadcast of the Christos wave, and the resulting static shows up as anger, hatred, greed and grievances. The particles will give form to any wave. That is the Law. The particles define Spirit. Spirit reveals Itself in this dimension through the aid of particles or what is commonly called matter. The first thing for us to realize is that we are Spirit and that Spirit is Love.

Spirit as Form

There is no form without Spirit and no Spirit without form. If God is everywhere present, then God is present in form. The form we as Spirit give to relationships is a choice. If our choice is holy or whole, we have channeled the complete wave. We have expressed what God wants, which is Love. Anything less than Love is an incomplete wave, and the form it takes will be unloving.

The light as God is Love and Intelligence expressing through Law. It is Spirit. Mystics, philosophers, saints, sages and some scientists now say matter is only a shadow, or a nothing (no thing). Matter does not exist in and of itself. There is a power called Spirit that brings "life" or definition to form. The Spirit as us gives definition to form by the way we think, what we say, and what we do. To that extent we are co-creators with the Almighty. The Spirit as us makes unenlightened or enlightened choices. Through the power of our mind we distort the wave through unenlightened choices. Through the power of our mind we can select what God wants.

Love as a Vibrational Wave

The wave God the Father makes is Love. That wave cannot be created or destroyed. It is the everlasting Truth of our being. God the Mother is impregnated with Love and is constantly giving birth to Its vibrations. The feminine aspect of God is always giving birth and nurturing the seed or the word of God (masculine aspect of God) into expression. Our soul, psyche, or mind is an individualization of Divine Mind. Our infundibulum brings the whole Love waves into our subconscious mind. Our modem is connected to Eternal Love. Our soul or mind positions itself through prayer, meditation and selfless service to receive the direct impress, or impulse, known as Love.

Power in Choice

The law of our being receives the direct wave in the fertile womb of our subconscious mind. Our conscious mind chooses to bring Love into the world of form. The forms of our thoughts are things. The things we produce on the screen of life correspond to the way we think. Our activities manifest through the power of choice. Fear-motivated choices produce static and make incomplete waves. Whole waves resemble Love. Love is cooperative with what God wants, whereas fear is competitive with what God wants. Love has no opposition other than ignorance. Ignoring what God wants is not the correct position or focus for our thoughts. Ignorance is horizontal thinking. We are operating our personal computers with a self-directed, limited focus.

The Meaning of Revelation

Knowing what God wants and expressing It is revelation. We position our minds to work in concert with the Divine Mind. Our personal computer is linked. The vertical channel is open. The vertical thoughts are undistorted, static-free, whole waves. It is the Christos, the Christ light within, revealing Truth. We understand what Love is and we express It. Our minds, souls and psyche are focused on Love.

The Christ-like person becomes less interested in form and more interested in Spirit. More interested in the wave, less interested in the particle. More interested in vertical thoughts, less interested in horizontal thinking. The words that God the Father within speaks are Light, Wholesome, and Holy. They are Love. If we act in concert with God, we channel Love. We come up with the right answer and fulfill the Law. That is the ultimate revelation.

The Law Works Horizontally

Law is like the principle of mathematics. We cannot see the principle but we can use it either correctly or incorrectly. We can understand how the Law works, what it does, and how to use it. The Law of mathematics, properly used, allows us to bring wonderful and beautiful things into form—like houses, buildings, roads, planes, satellites and art forms. The thoughts we give to relationships are just as real as the material things we build. The visible expression of what we create allows us to see the results of our application and understanding of the Principle. The particles reveal the thought forms as our experience. Whatever we think, whatever we give our mind to, becomes materialized. The Law operates on the horizontal plane. It has no choice; it will reflect back to us exactly what we give our attention, our focus, to.

A Wonderful Key

Jesus gave us a wonderful key. He modeled, lived and identified with Love and Truth. He affirmed Love and fulfilled the Law of being. He did not find fault with Peter or Judas for being fearful or ignorant or ambitious at His expense. He appealed to the crowd and stopped the capital punishment of Mary Magdalene. When Peter became frightened and cut the ear off the soldier, Jesus asked him to put his sword away; and Jesus as the Christ healed the ear. His clairvoyant faculty allowed Him to perceive future events. His human nature, His horizontal thinking, preferred not to suffer the crucifixion. He preferred not to go through this extreme and painful punishment, but His vertical alignment, however, knew this was the will of the Father within.

Alignment with what God wants results in healing the sick, mending the broken-hearted, releasing the prisoner from the bondage of horizontal thinking. Horizontal thinking without the leaven of Love is fear-driven. We place our faith in the material, or the particles, and of themselves they are *no thing*.

Jesus disciplined Himself to reveal what God wants. His consciousness funneled Love as a wave or vibration that was completely vertically aligned. The resurrection is evidence that the wave or Spirit cannot be destroyed. Life goes on, life is a continuum. The particles lighten up as we cooperate with Spirit. Our true self is Spirit. To know God is to know Self as Love.

"We are indeed born for Love. Love makes for exhilarating study, for only in the act of loving are we sufficiently distracted from ourselves to view, even momentarily, a glimpse of our true self," says Leo Buscaglia.

The Lady in the Laundromat

There was a young man sitting next to me in a laundromat in England waiting for the laundry cycle to finish. I asked him if I could borrow a pen. The rather tall, slender young man wearing blue jeans and a loose-fitting plaid shirt turned out to be a young lady from Germany.

I had interrupted her meditative experience. She responded with kindness, however, and said that as she was watching the clothes and soap move rhythmically her mind (through her heart) reflected upon happy times in childhood. She remembered when her parents got their first washing machine with a glass window in the door. It was an enjoyable family event, watching the machine go through its cycles. She was keeping her mind on lovely things, not the evil things, that were done in Germany. Love requires a disciplined mind. A mind that has learned to focus consciously on Love lightens up.

This young German woman's name is Christiana. She learned the value of meditating on the good in a spiritual community in Findhorn, Scotland. She also learned to be a masseuse. She knows that she is a channel for God's love. As we consciously identify with Love, we come nearer to expressing that we are Spirit as Love. Christiana disciplined her mind to think in a Love-conscious way. As Christiana did her massage work, she would stay centered on Love, and light would channel through her, as her. Dr. Thomas Hora would call her a "beneficial presence." Christiana was cooperating with Love and expressing Truth.

(Love is kind. Love is true. Love seeks no evil.)

Drummond would ask, "Do we have the feeling and conviction of God's abiding presence wherever we are?" Christiana found joy in a laundromat. She feels she radiates joy in her work. Getting her ego out of the way often requires work. She revealed to me, "I do better work when I don't try to take personal credit for the work I do. I am not always successful. Sometimes I take personal credit or blame myself, and I feel separated from my Source. I do what I can to bring Love into everything I do.''

(Love is not puffed up or vaunteth itself. Love is humble.)

Joy and Peace are soul qualities that are obvious to the observer of Christiana's expression.

"The real sign that God, the Giver of Life, has been received into our souls will be joy and peace: joy, the spirit of selfless delight; peace, the spirit of tranquil acceptance; the very character of the beatitudes of Heaven'' (from the writings of Evelyn Underhill).

Love Does Not Discriminate

There seems to be an increased number of souls that are tuning in to funnel consciousness. We are becoming more aware of what God wants. Divine Love is indiscriminate. It delights in the allness of Spirit. "God loves, not tolerates, these wayward, half-grown, self-centered spirits, and seeks without ceasing to draw them into His Love,'' says Underhill. So there we have it. Divine Love neutralizes egos and heals fear.

Love Is Ageless

Love is an everlasting soul quality that is timeless. It just needs to be remembered and chosen in order to be realized. Remember the reply of the five- and seven-year-old boys. . . . "Love is marriage, sex. Love is friendship. Love is being together, dancing, having girl friends. Love is helping. I felt very mad and that's not Love." How brilliantly and simply spoken out of the mouth of a child. The emphasis is, *LOVE IS*. A few moments later the seven-year-old entered the room and said, "The specialest love in the world is the Love of everything."

Who Needs to Write?

Who needs to write a book on Love? The fathomless quality of Love is imprinted on the soul . . . funneled through the infundibulum, if you wish. Love is waiting to be recognized and expressed. Love expresses through us as we accept It and fulfill our purpose for being here. Why do I write this book? Because I feel an inner compulsion to express Truth as I understand it. I can't give you Truth; you already have it. The encouraging words I write and the stories I tell are my endeavor to express Love. How *you* individualize Love is *your* business. Denying the Love that impels us to be uniquely us is not a viable option.

O God, hear our cry, let the immortal
splendor of our Soul place its vested
interest in Thee;
Denounce the fear that was never meant to be.
Impress us with Thy Love, and let us see,
the influx of Thee in we.

C. Sommer

Opening the Clairvoyant Channel

Henry Drummond instructed his students in this way to open the channel of spiritual discernment: "Look upon this shadow long and earnestly, till that which you look through becomes the shadow, and the shadow merges into reality. Look through till the thing you look through becomes dim, then transparent, and then invisible. The unseen beyond grows into form and strength. For, truly the first thing seen is the shadow, the things on the other side the reality (that which is Real). We are to pass through it as clairvoyants, holding the temporal world as a vast transparency, through which the eternal shines." (*Clairvoyant* comes from two root words meaning "to see clearly.")

Modern-day physicists realize that the particle and the wave are inseparable. The properties of one can be observed in the other, as though there is only one. No matter how deeply we explore outer or inner space, we cannot penetrate the vastness of the Eternal. Yet something in us knows Itself to be One. There is an in-

definable unity in diversity—which is another way of
saying we are one in Spirit.

To know God is to know the One. To express Love is
to be Christ-like. It has been said, ''The only sin is a
mistake, the only salvation is Love.''

Confronting Fear

It is not familiarity that breeds contempt; *we* do. It is our
lack of patience or our choosing to be rude rather than
gentle. The spoiled child has not yet emerged into the
gentle man or woman.

As I write these words, I am recording an event that
just happened. And remember, there are no accidents.
Every moment has its opportunity to choose Love. Here
is the event that just happened. I am a guest, using a
semiprivate office in a secretarial pool of women. A very
loud voice screams out, ''Whoever is sending out faxes
is driving me mad. The phone keeps ringing in my ear.''

It was at that moment that I realized it must be my
phone. I was calling an airline that is experiencing financial difficulty and is understaffed. I was letting the phone
ring for five minutes. I had the volume ring very low on
my speaker phone, and I could hardly hear the ring, but
somehow the noise bled through to the phone in the ad-
joining office.

Although I don't much like confronting angry persons,
I pressed through the fear of rejection and said, ''It must

be my phone. I am sorry. I was unaware that the noise was bleeding through!'' The young lady was very embarrassed that she had yelled out. "I would not have done it if I knew it was you. Look at my face, it is red. I should be more patient. I should keep my mouth shut.'' We can all see ourselves in her. We often say things we later regret. I asked her if she would mind if I gave her a little advice. She reluctantly nodded her head no. I then suggested to her that rather than choosing anger or holding her frustration in by not saying anything, she might try this: As she began to feel her blood boil with frustration, ask herself gently: "What can I do to resolve this frustration peacefully?''

(Love is kind to oneself and others)

Drummond called this type of behavior the disease of "touchiness.'' Let us ask ourselves, do we like to be around touchy people? If our answer is no, then something in us knows that the only "touchy" person that we can heal is within ourselves. The eternal light of timeless reality shines through the fabric of mortal expression, showing Itself as Love.

The Formula for Happiness Is Simple

The formula for addition and subtraction is simple. However, to apply the formula and get the correct answer requires work. Spirit can only work through us, as us. The enlightened choice is to cooperate with Spirit. Here is what St. Paul suggests. "Do not be anxious about anything" (Philippians 4:6). "Rejoice in the Lord always." He could have said: "Fear not, rejoice in Truth."

Notice with me that, when we are anxious, it is our ego's vested interest in the fabric, in the form. To see the humor in the web we weave is a precious gift of Love that cannot be contained by fear. Which brings me to a marvelous story I have held in reserve until now. It is *our* story.

Love Is Courageous

In some individuals, intuition is more developed than in others. That is all right, because there are no mistakes in Law. The Law works with mathematical certainty, and it is the sum and substance of all that precedes it. We are all ordained or anointed by God to play our part in the scheme of things. God loves each one of us. It is the realization of Love that brings us home. I met a courageous woman minister in Anchorage, Alaska, whose inner beauty matched the conviction of her heart to follow the inner nudge, to do what she deemed was right, to put anxiety aside and muster together the force of Love, a force that takes us to new frontiers within ourselves.

As we courageously honor the Spirit within, we courageously go forth in the world as a beneficial presence. Remember, this is *our* story. The name does not matter. Rev. Polly C. Dozier is short in stature, yet vibrant with a soft but firm voice. She has raised her family and is now called upon to serve the global family beyond the confines of her church. She is deeply motivated to serve God, this planet and humanity.

The inner call she got was to go to Russia. Rev. Polly knew she would be involved in doing spiritual work there, but had no clue as to what or where or with whom. Rev. Polly knew from many prior experiences to trust God and to take one step at a time, listening and following her internal guidance. It often requires courage to go into an area with political and military unrest. This act of courage was not so much a leap of faith as it was an abiding loyalty to follow the prompting of her intuition.

Her Anchorage church members put together a fundraiser to sponsor her trip, along with other friends who provided additional financial support for her trip to Russia.

When she landed in Moscow in November of 1990, Polly had no clue as to what her next move would be, but she trusted in Spirit to guide her. She did a few tourist things while she waited for the next nudge. She knew she must be patient, for Spirit works through humility, not willfulness.

(Love is patient and humble)

The nudge came the next day. She thought she was going to Kiev, a large city in the Ukraine, but through the encouragement of some of her friends and a businessman's insistence, she decided to take a train to a small town called Kirov. The intuitive flash, the inner know-

ing, said *go*. The long and arduous journey took her to
a remote area usually restricted to outsiders. She was in
for a big surprise: Kirov turned out to be a 600-year-old
city of half a million people. It was also a city off-limits
to tourists because secret military devices were made
there.

Rev. Polly was taken to a church house where she was
introduced to a Russian Orthodox Archbishop. Much to
her amazement, the Archbishop had been waiting for
her. His intuition had somehow provided him with the
information that a woman priest from the United States
of America would come to help him. He truly had been
waiting for her arrival. Rev. Polly's and the Archbishop's
inner knowing, directed by Love, drew these two unlikely
players together in a cosmic dance.

The dance went like this: Rev. Polly, with the help of
an interpreter, found herself assisting the Archbishop
with a religious service that was foreign to her in form but
not in Spirit. The customs, the language, the people were
no barrier to Love. The people were happy to have her
there as they jointly exercised religious freedom publicly.
She had not come there to convert. She was there to
assert a human right that springs from the eternal.

(Love rejoices in Truth)

The few days she was in Kirov, Rev. Polly was not
given the keys to the city, but rather became the key to
the cooperation of opposing forces. Under Soviet rule the
government had taken possession of all the church properties and used them for state purposes. The Soviet

government had prosecuted and persecuted those who would not give up their religious practices.

Polly was informed that the governor was willing to meet the Archbishop only if Polly would act as a facilitator. Polly's first reaction was not to get involved in someone else's problems. She decided to meet first with the very troubled Archbishop who deeply resented the oppression by the state. He confessed to her his deep-seated anger. She was nonjudgmental about his anger, his hurt, his suffering. She had become the priest that he was looking for, although she had not considered herself a priestess. In a loving, confrontational way, like a Zen master, petite Rev. Polly confronted the large, powerful Archbishop and instructed him to forgive and let go of the painful past.

(Love does not behave unseemly or rejoice at iniquity)

The Archbishop, the Governor and Rev. Polly met together. The men began to talk Russian and Polly understood and talked through an interpreter. All of a sudden the room was filled with laughter. It was explained to Polly that the Governor asked the Archbishop this question, ''Where does Rev. Polly, a young minister, get all her wisdom?'' The Archbishop told him she had been in training since the age of twelve. That, they found funny. Polly had recently told the Archbishop that she had an enlightening experience at age twelve, an experience that brought her into the awareness that she would be a minister.

The meeting continued, and the portal to constructive communications was reopened after decades of closure. The resentment barriers came tumbling down. Progress came slowly but surely at this first meeting. The second meeting came about eight months later when Polly returned to Kirov once again from Alaska. This time, there were press conferences, TV interviews, meetings with the mayor and the Archbishop. The former church properties were gradually being given back. The wounds of many generations were being healed. The channel of viable communication was now open. How marvelously Rev. Polly was used as a channel for reconciliation. Little did she know that the Father within would use her to build a bridge of Love in a distant land, or a foreign place. But no place is foreign to Love. Love is Truth and it is everywhere, just as the invisible wave is everywhere. We can become the catalyst between the particle and the wave that makes Love obvious. Then Love takes form through us.

(Love is Truth)

Healing Presence

In my travels from Anchorage, Alaska, to Mexicali, Mexico, linking with spiritual teachers, one thing became more apparent than ever: the importance of listening to feeling, and understanding spiritual guidance. I do not mean listening to discarnate entities that may lead us into the dark side of the force but rather to the guidance coming from God-directed Holy Spirit. The White Brotherhood, Ascended Masters, saints and sages, archangels, the Holy Madonna, Jesus the Christ, the Buddha are all instruments of the Most High. They serve the omnipresence of the Lord God Almighty. Each of them and each of us who follow the example of turning to the Father within, surrendering to all that Is, receives true empowerment.

Empowerment by the Holy Spirit nurtures us to see, to feel, to know the Good in all. The Word of God comes through us, as us. We are vessels. Our cargo is Love. Love is the healing agent. We are Its messengers on this planet Earth. The message is: Christ is in the Father, and we in Christ. We are One in Spirit. Our minds teach us to differentiate but Love teaches us to be inclusive, to unify, to endure all things. Love from God is generously portioned to the meek (*"meek"* meaning the ability to return good for evil, to effectively practice nonresistance). The renewing of the mind makes differentiation less important, because Love is the ultimate answer. Love is an energy that never separates; rather it unifies. Love is energy that cannot be created or destroyed. Love uses us, and we use It. We can never be separated from Love although we may be unaware of Its presence.

(Love believeth all things and hopeth all things)

We can feel as though there were no Love in our lives. We can feel separated from our Source. We can despair. But Love is still there, though we may be ignorant of it. Ignorance is the only sin. The pain of separation is healed by true Love. Love—expressing through a medical doctor, through a Soul doctor, through a spiritual healer, through a nurse, through the patient—is the healing balm. We can use Spirit, plasma or herbs. We can use acupuncture, chiropractic, surgery, psychotherapy, and so forth and so on. We can hypnotize or dramatize. "LIVING LOVE IS THE MOST DYNAMIC HEALING ACTIVITY." Ignorance is the veil hiding Love realization.

We can chant, meditate and pray. We can affirm or deny Love. True Love can never corrupt. It is not egotism. It is self-realization. Losing ourselves in God is finding ourselves in Spirit. I call that Spirit *Love*.

The healing facilitators whom I most admire serve God most of all. They realize Love in their work, deeds and activities. We who are served by them are twice blessed. We can only acknowledge Love in another when realizing It within ourselves. That is the double blessing.

Most of us in the healing arts are learning how to administer love. The inspirational form it takes depends on how well we respond to guidance. Humility is the portal through which the Light as God reveals Itself to us in fullness. HUMILITY: HU means Light, as in hue; MILITY means soldier—a soldier of Light in the service of Spirit as Spiritual Being, in accordance with the Law of our being. A Christ-centered being recognizing Love has an impulse to act in a beneficial way. The form of the act is up to us. One Power, One Mind, provides the inspiration, the perspiration and the dissemination. That is to say, God provides all; He gives us the Intelligence, the energy, and the means to distribute Love in whatever form we choose. The rest is up to us. God can only do *for* us what God can do *through* us.

The actor Anthony Hopkins (*Silence of the Lambs*) admitted in a television interview that he was a hopeless drunk. Through an expression of humility, he asked for help. He cried out for help to a power greater than himself. (That is true humility.) He got an immediate answer and an instant cure. He experienced an act of faith, a rush of energy, a feeling of well-being, a glow of light, an innner voice, a peaceful assurance. Anthony is most grateful for the experience. He is uncertain what to call this *power*, this *divine* presence. He thought it might be God! What would you call It?

I call It God . . . God individualized through an expression of humility. Anthony uttered a primordial cry to an Infinite Spirit, which answered as Love Itself. God always answers our calls whether we hear them or not. God is so infinitely good and generous. But we get the messages through our infundibulum only when we are ready.

(Love is generous)

PART V

Love: How to Expand It

We have discussed many facets of Love. How to recognize It in ourselves and others. How It works according to law as a Divine Presence. What It does through us, as we are open to It. How to cooperate with It, as It. And finally, now, how to expand It.

> One of the holy miracles of Love is that once It is really started on Its path, It cannot stop: It spreads in ever-widening circles till It embraces the whole world in God. We begin by loving those nearest us, end by loving those farthest. And as our Love expands, so our whole personality will grow, slowly but truly. Every fresh soul we touch in Love is going to teach us something fresh about God.
>
> Evelyn Underhill, *Immanence*

Nothing Happens by Accident

Nothing happens by accident. There is an unerring law of cause and effect. We do not have to be great spiritual leaders or scientific pundits to grasp the law of cause and effect. Simply put, it means that like begets like.

Some people radiate a great deal of Love. A friend was telling me that she was in a large audience of well-dressed women in Beverly Hills listening to Leo Buscaglia. The audience was so moved by Love that many of them began to cry tears of joy. Professor and author, Dr. Buscaglia is very creative in his methods of instruction and counseling students. Love is most creative when we honor Its presence in our lives.

Love and Law always work in concert. Through God's Love, we can imagine and create any kind of thought. Through God's Law, thoughts will always express. Thoughts are things, and that is one reason why we can feel or pick up the unverbalized expression. Law is like a double-edged sword. If we are feeling antagonistic, everyone around us psychically feels it. If you walk into a room where people won't speak to each other, you can feel the wall of anger. It is simple to understand and to feel how the Law works.

If the presence of God is Love and Law, it is also simple to prove it. The Law is always producing our thoughts. What we put our mind to, what we focus on, shows up. Something in us gives energy to thoughts—call it the Law, call it focus. And we are given the power to change our thinking, but such change requires interest and discipline. I can't prove to anyone that Love is the greatest thing in the world—I can only prove it to myself. No one else can do it for me. I either *act* out of Love or *react* out of fear.

The Minister Chose Fear

A woman in her mid-fifties, whom I'll call Jan, recently discovered that her father was not her biological father. In fact, her mother divorced her biological father when she was an infant. The natural parents swore that they would never tell that they were divorced or that he was the father. Because the biological father was a part-time orthodox minister, he feared that he would lose his ministry if his followers knew that he was divorced. His fears of suffering the loss of his ministry caused him to live a lie. He thought he could avoid suffering the consequences of living a lie, but in fact, it cost him loss of self-respect, and it cost him the loss of a daughter that he never knew.

Sometimes it takes a lot of courage to tell the truth. We tend to give in to fear, to find fault with others, and to place blame on those who make the same mistakes that we are covering up. We ministers are continually struggling to find the Christ within ourselves. Christ is Love, but fear obstructs our focus. The Holy Comforter is Truth, Light and Love, and Truth and Love will eventually surface.

In the case of Jan, the truth was finally brought out some 55 years later when she discovered the original marriage certificate stored away in her mother's house. Jan went to the library and other places to do research. Through her research, Jan found two half-sisters and the widow of her biological father.

(Love rejoiceth in Truth)

Jan did not wish to startle them by announcing her existence over the phone, and so she wrote to them. She immediately got a call from one of her half-sisters, who was disturbed by the news. The half-sister conducted her own investigation to be certain Jan was telling the truth. Then the half-sisters confronted their mother, and the mother reluctantly told them the truth. The mother was angry that Jan had spoken with them. She wanted to be the one to inform (or not inform) her two daughters.

(Love envieth not and is kind)

Fear Is Reactive

So, we can see that fear is reactive. We often lie because we are afraid of the reaction of others. The minister was afraid to lose his church followers. Since he preached against divorce, he—as a divorced person—would look bad. He feared he would suffer some unwanted consequences, like getting fired from his part-time job. We ministers will often project what we consider our hidden sins onto others. We will rebuke other brothers and sisters for falling from grace and getting a divorce. The truth is we have fallen from grace when we lie. Our cover-up perpetuates the problem. The solution is telling the truth, for Love is Truth. Asking for forgiveness and telling the truth will reopen the infundibulum and allow grace and inspiration to flow through.

Love Is Omni-Active

Love is courageous. Love is the activity of Spirit. Spirit and Love are omniactive and omnipresent. Love is not reactive, for it is the activity of God, and God does not react to Itself. God has nothing to cover up or hide. God can't know fear, for God is Truth. Therefore to know God is to know and express Truth.

Love is always present, like the wave and the particle. The wave requires particles of Truth in order to become visible. Choosing Truth and expressing it are usually acts of Love. However, telling the truth so as to blame and shame someone else is not kind. That is not Love. Telling the truth to expose some iniquity requires courage.

The television program ''60 Minutes'' endeavors to investigate and bring out truth and shed light on matters that are important to humanity. That is kind. That is courageous. I'm sure ''60 Minutes'' has been threatened many times by economic interests that see the ''bottom line'' as their god. If ''60 Minutes'' were to hold grievances rather than seek Truth, it would not be Love. ''60 Minutes'' may not be lily white; they too have their critics. Yet to those of us who have something to hide, it may not appear to be kind to have someone expose our cherished lie. Organizations that perpetuate lies to cover up abuses to our brothers and sisters for their own economic gain view truth as a threat. The world of race consciousness would have us believe that Truth is a threat. Truth is not the threat—the lie is the threat. Love has nothing to cover up.

(Love endureth all things for the sake of Truth, even suffering in this world)

Our Covenant with God

We males often are afraid of being too sentimental or emotional. We have been conditioned not to own our true feelings. As a result we have suppressed, constricted and depressed the life force. We pretend that we are insensitive, because we are afraid our peer group will think us soft. We deny the warmth and gentleness of who we are. In so doing we have broken the agreement with God to express our true selves.

Many men and women today are growing into the awareness that it is important to be a gentle, kind and considerate person. This kind of attitude keeps our covenant with God to love God and one another as much as our own self. Love is an activity of wholeness. As we love, our experience of It expands. Love is expansive. As we express Love, we enrich the world with our presence, for Love is the presence of God, and there is no greater gift than Love and no greater Joy than expressing It. Leo Buscaglia says, ''When we are truly loving, we become a part of a growing union of lovers whose strength comes from gentleness and whose example is in selfless treatment of others. When we become active in this special union, we are forever enhancing and we are never alone.''

Love Is a Holy Instant

At times, we all can take ourselves too seriously. God, help me lighten up when I am too serious. A few days ago it was New Year's day. The supermarket was busy, and I was in a hurry. Sometimes it seems as if everyone is too slow when I'm in a rush, and everyone is going too fast when I want to slow down and look for exact change, or make time to be social. When I get impatient, it is usually at things and events that are out of my control. Yet, surrendering control and giving up judgments are actions that, frankly, I am not good at—then I miss discovering the joy in the moment.

I was quickly counting my change at the checkout stand to make room for the next person in line. The next person was an older, modestly dressed black lady who wished the cashier a Happy New Year. What a wonderful and simple gesture. The cashier beamed a smile from what was otherwise a sullen face. ''Life is not too short but there is always time for courtesy,'' wrote Ralph Waldo Emerson. This kind gesture was a holy instant—it was filled with Love.

Cosmic Consciousness

We may not agree with choices that others make; however, we can respect the power within them that conceived their choices. Unwanted, undesired, and painful experiences have as much Love in them as pleasurable ones. If we understand that God is Love, and that Love is fundamental to everything, we can then conclude that God is present even in those who disagree with us or spitefully use us. As an ordinary person, it may be difficult for us to understand what St. Paul meant when he said, "All things work together for good." As we practice Love, it becomes more apparent that our understanding is growing. Our concerted effort brings Love to light.

We each can access universal awareness through our infundibulum. Actually, God's presence is everywhere. As we awaken to God in our innermost part, we discover God in the outermost part. Emerson says this in "The Informing Spirit": "There is no great and small to the Soul that maketh all; And where it cometh, all things are: And it cometh everywhere." God makes Itself known through Love and Law. There is something in us that knows there is a cosmic harmony to all events. Something in us knows *when not to interfere*. For example, Jesus did not give orders or even request that Peter not deny recognizing Him. Jesus even supported Judas' choice to betray him. He said, "Be quick about your business." Jesus, through the use of His expanded consciousness, realized that Love was working in this otherwise very negative experience—being betrayed by a disciple for money.

Make No Judgments against One Another

Ernest Holmes said, "I have seen no person healed unless there came a time when he knew the Universe had no judgments against him or he against anyone else: he returned to the simple basis of the givingness of Self, the recognition of the divine Presence in everything." Perhaps the Beatles' best song was "All You Need Is Love." I am convinced, more than ever, the best choice is always Love. Ralph Waldo Emerson said, "Give all to Love; Obey thy heart; . . . 'Tis a brave master; Let it have scope: Follow it utterly; Hope beyond hope."

Jesus the Christ, the Example

Jesus, the greatest example of Love, never claimed to be an exception. Jesus often asked, "Who do you say I am?" Two thousand years ago the prevailing thought placed God outside of us. It was considered blasphemy to identify with God. Jesus, the master teacher, knew that we were made in the image and likeness of God and that, if we followed His example, we too would come to know the Father within.

We can choose to fulfill the law of our being by obeying the will of God, Allah, Abba, Adonai, Elohim, Iśvara, Buddha, the Thing Itself. Let us not be confused by the many names for God. Make it simple. God is Love; God is Law. Love is a gift, not a possession; the

Law is simple: effect follows cause. Through the grace of involution, Love is the perfect gift—a gift which is always there waiting to be recognized and expressed. We each have this gift inherent in us. In order to realize the gift, though, we must express it.

Love Is the Only Choice

I never met Ernest Holmes in person, but I feel that his works are profound. He successfully endeavored to give us a broader theology that puts fear and superstition where they belong. He grasped the kernel of Truth like many others before him. He said, ''I don't think we should be afraid. I think the beginning of wisdom is not the fear of God but the knowledge, the Love, the worship, the adoration, the sense of divine Presence.'' Ernest Holmes' greatest legacy to us is his teaching of affirmative prayer.

Ernest Holmes, near the end of his earthly life, gave a seven-minute talk that made an impact greater than any of the other numerous talks he had given during his 40+ years as a teacher. This talk was given to a large group of strangers in a hotel conference room. What made the difference? He used affirmative prayer. He affirmed that he was Love, that everyone in his audience was Love. He was not afraid to identify with God. God is Love. What he could accept for himself, he could accept for others.

Jesus and others have repeated the same key. Love

God, love self, love one another. More than 40 years of practice at affirming Truth brought Holmes into a deep and great realization that living Love is the dynamic answer.

Creative Living

Creative living requires sacrifice. We have to be willing to give up fear, which is not an easy task. We have to be willing to forgive ourselves and others for the moments in which we reacted from fear. Fear is always a reaction to something that seems to be threatening our security. Love is at the center of all creativity. Love is not a reaction—It is the only *action*. It is an activity of Spirit, and It actively expresses through us as we affirm it. As we identify with Love, It confirms Itself through us. This is the only way it can happen, for Love is the Law of our being.

Ability-to-Respond

Responsibility is nothing more than the ability-to-respond as Love. What does it mean to examine our conscience? Nothing more than this—in the moment of now, we simply ask ourselves: "Am I reacting from fear? Or am I actively expressing Love?" The more often we choose Love, the more our spiritual awareness grows and develops. Like Leo Buscaglia, Ernest Holmes, Henry

Drummond, Ralph Waldo Emerson and others, we too
can make a beneficial presence known. The presence of
Love is the presence of God. We have chosen God-
awareness in every moment that we respond as Love.
Love is always the intelligent choice.

Love is not separate from intelligence. Love is the most
creative of all. Can you think of anything new that did
not require letting go of the old? We are always discovering new frontiers in science, art, inner and outer space.
Love impels, compels and propels Itself through us. Let's
learn to cooperate with It. Each one of us is precious to
God. We are each students and teachers. What we are
here to learn and teach is Love. What form Love takes
in our life depends upon how well we receive the direct
impress of the Divine Will and how well we willingly
become Its instrument.

Cosmic Awareness

Many of the astronauts who have ventured into outer
space have developed great awe of the beauty and vastness of God. Many who have journeyed into inner space
have experienced *cosmic consciousness*. At the inception of
the twentieth century a wonderful doctor wrote a book
called *Cosmic Consciousness*. He was Richard Maurice
Bucke, M.D. He wrote, ''We have the intuitional . . .
the mind whose highest element is not a recept [recep-
tacle] or a concept but an intuition. This is the mind
in which sensation, simple consciousness, and self con-

sciousness are supplemented and crowned with *cosmic consciousness*. In this consciousness, like the apostle Paul, we see the Good in all.''

Dr. Bucke was the superintendent of an insane asylum in London, Ontario. There is a beautiful movie that can be rented on videotape called *Beautiful Dreamer*, released by Hendale. This movie shows how Dr. Bucke, a man of science, accomplishes more good through Love than through cold science. Walt Whitman, as portrayed by Rip Torn, became the catalyst, the example of Love in action for Dr. Bucke. Dr. Bucke, the psychiatrist, and Walt Whitman, the extraordinary humanistic nineteenth-century American poet and prophet, became good friends. Whitman lived from his heart, and his intellect responded with beautiful works. ''The poet feels that his Love is as irresistible and mystical as are the forces of nature. The self of the poet is shown floating on the open air, and this image suggests the mystical merger of man's soul with the Divine Soul,'' writes V. A. Shahane, Ph.D. He goes on to write about Whitman: ''He intuitively comprehends the great mysteries of life, birth, death, and resurrection and plays the part of a priest and a prophet for mankind.'' Dr. Bucke's career and lifestyle changed dramatically for the good when Love was introduced to him by one person—Walt Whitman. One cosmically aware person sparks another, when they are ready. Dr. Bucke was well-taught and became an exemplary teacher as well.

In Dr. Bucke's book, he describes the life of 43 persons who exemplified cosmic consciousness. The point is that cosmic consciousness is found everywhere. It is Love coming to the surface in a powerful expression of Itself. The love wave is being revealed by the particle in a particular experience. The vertical thought, as a love wave, is expressed through Law on the horizontal plane of understanding. It feels good, it is good. It is Love, the common denominator, making Itself known through us, as us. It is being born again to the Power and Presence of God.

Wake-Up Call

Cosmic awareness does not happen just anywhere, any place, or to anyone. There is evidence that this new era we have entered, called the Aquarian Age, is providing a wake-up call. Many people have become conscious and proactive of protecting the environment, aiding the homeless, feeding the starving masses of humanity, putting an end to disease and war. As the funnel to cosmic consciousness enlarges, we access an awareness to greater understanding. "I cannot be awake, for nothing looks to me as it did before, or else I am awake for the first time, and all before has been a mean sleep," says Whitman.

Many people have had a near-death experience, an out-of-body experience, or an altered-state experience that is a wake-up call to a greater sense of Self. Below the surface of ordinary understanding is experienced an undefinable unity, but not a uniformity. Spirit never makes exactly the same thing. Each one of us is individual and is equally important to God. Our desire to make ourselves *more* important or others *less* important is troublesome. Cosmic awareness lets us understand the Good in all. Being born again means our mind is renewed with our soul purpose for being here—to express Love. It is Love that renews our minds and values the diversity in life and in each other. It is Love that gives us the understanding and ability to value all the unique and important components in the fabric of the Almighty.

Contemplation and Affirmation

Contemplation and affirmative prayer are excellent tools to align our little wills with the divine will, opening the portal to the ever-present cosmic awareness and allowing us to feel the impulsion of Love compelling us to affirmative actions. "Faith worketh through Love," according to St. Paul. Impulsion and compulsion are the twin flames of Love. The impelling love wave is working in concert with the particle to reveal Itself through the activity of God in us, as us. "When the double movement of Transcendent Love, drawing inward to unity and fruition, and rushing out again to creative acts, is realized in you, [you are Dynamically Living Love]. You are to be a living, ardent tool with which the Supreme Artist works; one of the instruments of His self-manifestation, the perpetual process by which His Reality is brought into concrete expression," says Evelyn Underhill.

Model Teacher

One of my greatest teachers, Margarita, can neither read nor write. She works in a poor area of Mexico. She uses her clairvoyant and clairaudient gifts to heal the sick. She generously gives food, clothing and comfort to the poor. She has reeducated the educated. Yet she will be the first to tell you that she knows nothing. It is God that heals. It is God that provides. How does she know God? She knows God through contemplation, meditation, prayer, song and selfless service. She gives freely of the talents given to her and uses them as an instrument of Love. Margarita has no time for anger, sadness or disappointment. She does take time out to renew, to recharge and to revitalize.

"The soul's two activities of reception and donation must be held in balance, or impotence and unreality will result. It is only out of the heart of his own experience that man really helps his neighbor: and thus there is an ultimate social value in the most secret responses of the soul to grace," wrote Underhill.

4GODIAM

4GODIAM (For-God-I-Am): That is what my automobile license plate says. Whoever reads it thinks a profound truth. We are all here for God. To know, to serve, to understand, to love God is our challenge.

At the tire store yesterday, the manager said, "I like

your license plate. You could turn it around to say *God's for me.*" I agree with him. God *is* for us individually and also collectively.

Who and what are we? Who do you say we are? Perhaps we can agree with the biblical statement that says we are made in God's image and likeness. That likeness is Love. One might say, "My God is a vengeful god and I believe in an eye for an eye." That is limited, unawakened, unenlightened thought that perpetuates revenge. Out of our collective unenlightened global consciousness we encourage the paranoia of the Hitlers, Joe McCarthys, et al. Out of our arrogance, prejudice and hate come a focal point, from which a sinister leader emerges. Out of every good deed, out of every inspired thought, out of Love's activities more of the same are produced. The good seed brings forth the leadership expresssing the collective values. Light transforms the darkness. Love dispels the fear. The sinister side of us is *playing* God. The enlightened side of us is *expressing* God. The choice is always ours. Are we expressing God, or playing God?

Afraid to Show Love?

Love expands in us to the extent we discover and use it. Love is so powerful that it *makes no demands*. Love is so powerful that it *demands expression*. This may seem like a contradiction, yet Love is so powerful and fulfilling that it can't be contradicted. We don't make Love or God real; It *is* real. Love is a quality of eternality and is the infinite One that is everywhere. Fear is a finite expression of an incomplete realization of Love. When we think fearful thoughts, we have become too interested in the finite and need to regain our perspective of the eternal. Fear is living in the shadow of the Almighty. We do not fear God as we live in God's Spirit. St. Peter says, "If we live in Spirit, let us also walk in Spirit." The enlightened way is free of shadows. Love is the Almighty expressing Itself through us.

During many years of a fruitful marriage, the most comfortable way for me to express Love to my beloved wife was nonverbally. I would squeeze her hand gently three times. Each squeeze was a secret code representing a word. "I love you." It took me 25 years to give myself permission to say it out loud. Expressing Love verbally seemed strange at first. It still requires some effort for me to break through the fear of embarrassment and tell my three sons I love them.

God is helping me find the courage to tell the truth about Love. God showed me, in a guided meditation, symbols that told me something was missing in my life. Meditation was something that had been foreign to me. By the aid of a trained facilitator in a group setting, I was taken to the "Father" within. This wise being took the form of an ancient American Indian. The old wrinkled Indian handed me a gift, a small leather pouch. In the pouch was a green heart carved out of precious stone.

The message I got from the meditative visualization was that I had a hardened heart of stone. That was the way I interpreted it, yet the color green told me my heart was ready and poised to express life more fully. Green was the "go" sign, the sign of growth. (The green in plants gives us food and oxygen, implying I should give my self to the Self.) The *precious* stone was the gift of Love. The soft, brown leather pouch represented something of importance. Softness meant not hard, pliable. The color brown was like the earth crust giving birth to the needs within. So the overall message for me was to face my apparent fears by pressing through my self-imposed embarrassment with an act of Love.

One with God

"The meek shall inherit the earth." "The first shall be last, and the last shall be first." I interpret that to mean that if we put finite values ahead of what God wants, we are making a mistake. It takes inner calm, gentleness, and devotion to be Love's representative. To know what God truly expects of us is Intelligence. Expressing what God wants is Love. *One* with God is more than a majority. The totality of God is with us in Truth. Standing tall in spiritual being gives us the courage to be channels for the Almighty.

Our Part Is Vital

Of ourselves we can do nothing. Our willingness to be channels for God empowers us to be all that God in-

tends. The Law is servant to the Spirit. I believe God is
Love, God is Truth. It behooves me to understand It, to
seek It, to know It, and to express It. If Spirit works
through one of us It works through all of us. I often use
examples of myself and others to convey what I understand to be Truth. What I understand and express as
truth, however, may differ from what others regard as
truth.

Our part in the expression of Love and Truth is more
vital than we realize. A friend whom I'll call Renee is the
mother of two teenage boys. She told of an incident that
happened some eleven years ago that has helped her to
this day. She said, ''The evening when I first met you,
Charles, you drove me to my car and said something to
me that has helped me through many an illness.'' I asked
her to explain. She went on to say, ''I confided my con-
cerns to you about my young son who was running a high
fever at the time. You told me that *God* often *provides* high
temperatures to burn away the infections and *not to worry*.
You said *Spirit is more intelligent and loving than we realize.*
Charles, you helped me get a broader understanding, a
realization that has helped me on many occasions over
the years.''

I explained to Renee that I simply expressed Truth as
I realized it that evening many years ago. ''I'm just a
channel,'' I told her. She said, ''I appreciate the channel'' and gave me a big hug. I looked to see if her husband approved of the hug; he did. We both did.

Now let me tell you about a young girl of fourteen that
I admired through the writing of Mark Twain; her name
is Joan of Arc.

Joan of Arc at a young age intuitively knew God desired to use her for a channel to bring a long, drawn-out war to an end. Out of humility, expressed as Love, she obeyed. It is hard to imagine a young teenage girl becoming a general of anything. However, Joan led troops into battle many times. She herself never injured anyone, even in the heat of battle. Yes, she was injured, betrayed, and later burned. God gave her the power to end a war. God gave her the power of intellect, the power of words, the sword of Truth. As her body burned, she forgave those who burned her. She expressed the courage and compassion of a Christ-like person.

(Love is courageous, generous and thinketh no evil)

Every unselfish act of Love fuels the winds of change with the calm breath of the Almighty. An instrument of peace is environmentally safe for earth. A channel for Love is the answer to the call within. Our part is vital to the universal good. Holy we stand; courageously we act. Our lives make a statement. We Love Pilgrims know our purpose.

(Living Love is the answer)

Fear Impedes Progress

Individuals often are frightened of expressing new ideas. We are afraid to buck the established system. Yet the waves of progress are filled with inspired people who endured much. They were not held back by such expressions as ''Don't fix it unless it is broke,'' ''Don't rock the boat,'' ''Don't make trouble,'' ''Don't make waves.'' At a human level, most institutions and individuals like to feel secure in the established ways. Then the divine nudge interrupts our ''status quo.'' The divine nudge is at work prompting us to enlarge our viewpoints, to expand our horizons in ways that are beneficial for the common good of all.

The Body Is a Vehicle

A wonderful man of science, an astute student, and a teacher of change was Joseph Campbell. He and his interviewer, Bill Moyers, gave us a fabulous look at ''The Power of Myth.'' A series of public television broadcasts brought us the inspirational history of humankind entitled ''The First Storyteller.'' It is an objective view that is an outgrowth of the subjective power within us all, the god-power individualized, realized, appreciated, and expressed. Campbell showed us the significance of metaphorically identifying with life.

Campbell said, ''The body is a vehicle of consciousness. Consciousness can watch consciousness join consciousness.'' What did he mean? He explained it another way. He told us metaphorically to identify with the Christ in us, to identify with the Shiva, the God within. He said we don't need a metaphorical image of God. If we just relax and identify with the Mind which moves everything, that opens the portal to inspired wisdom.

The term ''inspired wisdom'' reminds me of the story

an architect told me about himself some twenty years ago. I'll call him John. John said, "My high school mathematics teacher would give me a passing grade in order for me to graduate on only one condition. That condition was, I had to promise her never to take another math course." "John," I inquired, "how in the world did you become a structural engineer and architect with poor math skills?" He replied, "I learned the power of affirmative prayer from my grandmother who lived it and taught it. I prayed, knowing that God gives to all of us. And he certainly gave to me what I needed to know mathematically to serve as an engineer and architect. When I felt I was ready, I sat for the state exams and passed them. I obtained my certifications and licenses from the state without the necessity of going to college." Wow! I thanked John for his inspirational sharing and for his expert advice on an engineering challenge. John knew that God can give to us only what we can accept. Thank God John could accept for himself much more than his high school math teacher could (and she meant well). His math teacher was right in one respect: John did not have to take another math class to become what Spirit was urging him to be!

Old Mythology

God is all there is. There is no other. There is one mind, one life, one intelligence, one law. God does not need to be or desire to be feared. That is old mythology. There is no retribution outside the Law. The law of cause and effect is exacting and mathematically certain. We reap what we sow. What we do to others is done to us in the continuity of an endless life. Life is forever, and so there is no escape from the Law. But we need not fear the Law, for we can use the Law and cooperate with the Law. Our conscious choice must be to identify with God's presence within us, which we know to be Love. And Love always serves the greater Good.

(Perfect Love casts out fear)

Fear Creates Martyrs

It is fear of change that binds. It is our love of life in every moment of *now* that saves us. Almost every advancement in religion, science, business and the arts has its martyrs. A true martyr is inspired by God to bring forth the new, the beautiful, the good. When our orthodox values become intolerant, we shut down because we are fearful. Unreceptive to Love's call, we shut down our intuitive faculties. We often get lazy, set in our ways. But always, inspired thought is an internal idea waiting to be expressed, a truth waiting to be identified and lived.

Our projected fear is what creates the martyr. We collectively give power to a symbol of authority that commits an atrocity against our brother or sister. At all costs we feel we must maintain our status quo. But God does not forbid change. In fact, often it is through change that we grow. The only constant is the Law. The only Presence is Love, and Love—being dynamic—brings about change. Are we flexible enough to rise above fear and accept change?

Our Love creates the martyrs as well. There is something within us that has courage to act, to support and encourage the truth. It is our collective Love consciousness that breaks down the wall of ignorance, prejudice and animosity. It is our small acts of love that feed the divine potential. Established precedents then give way to the new. A leader, a savior, will transcend the bondage of limited thinking. Each of us has the capacity to transform and transcend limited beliefs because that Christ-like leader is God within us. We Love Pilgrims graciously accept Love as the transforming sovereign power.

Sovereign Power

Expressed Love forms a vortex of energy that knows no fear and has no boundaries. This God energy is in agreement with Love, Truth and Beauty. It resembles God, sovereign power at Its essence. We are not playing God out of a fear-driven mania. We are expressing God out of obedience to Divine will. Those of us who are awakening to God as Love wish to employ more of It, to become more God-like. It is not power itself that corrupts, but the misuse of it.

Love Is Not Bound by Precedent

In 1989, Rev. Barbara C. Harris, a black woman, became the world's first female Episcopal bishop. In a ceremony before 8,500 she was consecrated in Massachusetts, the church's largest diocese. The Episcopal Synod of America, led by Bishop Clarence Pope Jr., led a protest against the ordination and consecration of women. Popes and Pontiffs (derived from the Roman Latin root *pontifex*) are power positions of a male spiritual hierarchy that predates Christianity. At times, all of us—male and female—can be pompous or dogmatic in our beliefs. We can all abuse power for our own selfish interests.

Something in us knows that LOVE IS UNSELFISH. If something has no precedent, it does not mean it can't be done. It just means it has no precedent. To our limited knowledge, that particular thing has not been accomplished prior to now. Love is the energy that expands our way of seeing things, and an open heart reveals the Divine.

Divine revelation is as simple as a gentle nudge or as strong as a determination to express life fully, wholly and completely. How we interpret Love's impulsion depends on us. Not everyone gets a burning bush or an inner voice. As far as I'm concerned, anyone who is expressing Love is ministering what God wants.

I applaud individuals like Bishop Barbara Harris who endeavor to serve humanity in ways that are important to them. As all of us know, Love has no gender or hidden agenda. It is absurd to think that God is any less in a woman or any greater in a man. Every human life depends equally on male and female. God is Life. Love awakens us to life's fullness. Bishop Barbara C. Harris says, "I didn't come here to win a popularity contest. I came here to do the best I can with the gifts God has given me." Barbara does not expect you to kiss her ring. She is an activist for human rights, the divine right to express life fully. She marched with Martin Luther King. She works with prisoners. She is following Love's guidance within her.

Feminist Power

Feminist power was obvious in the ancient Gnostic and Cabala traditions, which appreciated women. Today, science has helped us realize that there are male and female traits in all of us. If Love, will, wisdom, knowledge, grace, power and beauty reside in one of us, the potential lies in all of us—male and female. We have women priests, rabbis, doctors, taxi-drivers, construction workers, governors, soldiers, scientists and mothers. The Law of Attraction, prompted by Love, makes us parents. The same creative urge encourages us to love God and one another. The same force gives all of us talents to use. It is up to us to discover and use them.

Successful Human Beings

"Successful human beings possess a combination of masculine and feminine traits. The most creative are a hybrid of supposedly conflicting characteristics: competitive and compassionate; goal-oriented and nurturing; intuitive and risk-taking. Cardboard, one-dimensional females and males alike are doomed to failure," say Patricia Aburdene and John Naisbitt, authors of *Megatrends for Women*.

Meditate on What?

Certainly the compassionate Buddha is another example of how Love expresses Itself through us. The Buddha was born a wealthy prince who later chose to suffer the life of an ascetic. He knew riches and poverty, pleasure and suffering. It was meditation that opened his funnel consciousness to the vastness of the Almighty and awakened him to express Love, in an enlightened way.

Observe our thoughts when we are worried and fearful. All we are expressing is anxiety. Observe our thoughts when we are happy. All we are expressing is joy. Meditation is choosing to focus our minds in the direction of Love and away from fear. It requires practice and discipline. St. Paul was teaching the people how to use their minds when he said, "I have learned, in whatsoever state I am, therein to be content" (Philippians 4:11). No one can change our thoughts for us—it's an internal job.

Meditation Is Choosing the Focus

Thinking on that which is beautiful, patient, kind, generous, humble, courteous and unselfish will produce a good temper. One of the benefits associated with developing a regular practice of meditation is quieting the mind. A quiet mind is most helpful in producing good temper. We must learn to be content in every situation. We can't always change the situation or circumstance but we can always change our minds . . . our attitudes. Remember, things come easy to those who practice. The bird that catches and rides the warm current of air to a greater height has had practice. As we practice focusing our mind on thoughts that we consider to be attributes of Love, we too soar to a greater awareness. We have left our worries behind and opened the channel to greater possibilities. By focusing our minds on Love's attributes, our creative faculty is open. Intuitive ideas provide answers that will work for us, as we put them to use.

(This is *The Dynamics of Living Love*)

Triune God

God creates everything out of Itself. I like to refer to God as a Triune God—the Father, the Mother (Holy Comforter) and the Child (the Son). I could have said it in scientific terms: God is Energy, Wave and Particle. I could have said it in terms of psychology: God is Superconscious Mind, Subconscious Mind and Ego. In terms of philosophy: God is Spirit, Mind and Matter. In terms of this book: God is Love, Law and Manifestation. In terms of us: God is desire, will and expression. There is no greater desire than to love, and there is nothing more powerful to express.

Suffering

In its early development, humankind thought we had to appease God or the gods by killing something—people, animals, each other. Thank God, many of us have evolved to understand there is something to sacrifice, but surely it is not each other. The ultimate thing to sacrifice is our sense of separation from our Creator. The battle takes place within ourselves. The next time we are angry, let's ask ourself these questions: What are we afraid of? What would Love do in this situation?

Fear Suppresses

One time I was very anxious about the possibility of failing a math class. My study partner turned to me and said, "Don't worry, in the long run it won't matter if you fail or pass." She was right. It helped release the tension. Leo Buscaglia has written that fear of failure causes many students to commit suicide at exam time. They are living life in a very narrow context. The broadest context is to be here for God as a channel of Love. God can help us change from being the channel for fear to being the channel for Love.

Many years later I was extremely anxious about the possibility of losing my home. A friend came to my rescue and said something absurd about real estate, and it got me laughing. I laughed so hard I fell off my chair and the roomful of people laughed with me (or at me).

When I was 27 years old, my Dad died. Through his death he gave me a wonderful gift. I went out in the street and cried. They were not tears of grief but tears of release. His death taught me that I had invested much energy in trying to please him. I had feared his rejection; I had wanted to win his approval. The tears released an emotional blockage that I did not realize I had. Another time, I was able to surrender a long-standing grievance I had against my brother, and again tears brought relief.

We can find something greater than channeling fear. And oh, what a relief to find It within ourselves. The true flame of Love burns up the fear of separation. It knows the self as One. True love cannot be created or destroyed. It just is.

Our psyche, moving from the finite to the infinite, struggles to purge ourselves of limited thinking, false beliefs and possessiveness. As we transfer our interest from self to God, our ego struggles, and a purification process brings us slowly into the greater Good. Now and again, we get glimpses of how God works in our lives, and the veil becomes very thin. Our souls, choosing to express Love even in the darkest hour, are pouring water on the seeming flame of separation. Underhill puts it this way, "This is the act of oblation [sacrifice] which puts life without condition at God's disposal; and so transforms and sacramentalizes our experience, and brings the Kingdom in."

Dark Night of the Soul

I like to give examples of real people like you and me. Our paths are uniquely individual, but the process is similar. Every account given in this book is real, even though I usually change the names to provide confidentiality to the individuals. Our egos would have us make something important of ourselves. Our Spirit would have us surrender ourselves to It. Ego-centered self-importance is not self-esteem; it is self-infatuation. Real power resides in Spirit. Nelson Mandela, Martin Luther King, Mahatma Gandhi, Mother Teresa, Jiddu Krishnamurti are twentieth-century examples of selfless service for the greater Good.

Each moment that we surrender to Love, we become Its instrument. Sometimes it may seem as if we are all alone in our choice to express Love. Love may ask us to surrender the comfort and stable circumstances we think we have in our possession. Possessions may be material, intellectual, interpersonal, psychic or emotional. What else is there? There is Love. Love is the liberator for those of us willing to serve It. Yes, we all err and fall back on false security. We are like unto the flower that closes itself into a bud during the dark of night, only to open ever fuller come the dawn, the light. As Eleanor Roosevelt said, "It is better to light a single candle than to curse the darkness."

Carol Karpeck is such a flower, whose fragrance of Love is shared with us now. With her permission, I now insert verbatim what she calls, "The Dark Night of the Soul."

The second major change came in 1991, when my physical world seemed to disintegrate: I lost my home to foreclosure, declared bankruptcy, and my business went into an apparently irreversible skid. No matter what I tried, dreamed, prayed for, I was left with only surrender. (Of course, I have since learned that surrender is the gift of freedom.)

I had been always an accomplished creator and controller in my own life, so I decided that I must have to surrender my business and find a full-time position working for someone else. I sent out resumes all over the country, seeking all types of work, without success.

During these 18 months—March 1991 to October 1992—I can accurately describe my experiences as the well-known *Dark Night of the Soul*. My logical, reasonable, creative mind that had never failed me, now seemed *impotent*. That was one word I used over and over— impotent—I had no sense of power on any level in my life.

Because of my despair, I sought escape in visions and dreams of the future. Anything to get me away from the horrible darkness in which I was forced to live.

I could plan for nothing, since I didn't know what God wanted me to do, much less what I wanted to do. I had always been so sure of my life's work as a teacher/trainer.

Now all I knew from my inner voice and the voices of psychics was that I am now a Healer. Of whom? With what? How? I had only questions of God and the Universe, including the basic human one: Why? Why me, God?

It has only been in the past month that I have come to answer those questions. GOD'S ANSWER IS (and always has been) LOVE! My answer is: Surrender to that Love.

And so, in September 1992, that is what I did. Surrendered totally to the Love in the now. No plans, no questions, no trying to force the Universe to follow my commands or timing. I just surrendered . . . and listened.

God's actions were immediate: For the first time in nearly a year, I received a call from a major company that wanted immediate and extensive training. And then another call . . . and another . . . I have been receiving contracts from new clients through referrals from previous clients, all without my direct intervention, all from Divine Love. And so, now I live fully in the Present, doing whatever I have in my life to do, with great Love and joy!

Carol's Living Love Formula
"*Surrender* = Freedom to Receive; Then *Give* = Love in Full Action"

Thank you, Carol, for sharing your experience and your new formula for Living Love. "Thank you, Charles, for honoring me and my wisdom," says Carol.

Wonders Never Cease

I enjoyed talking to a middle-aged man recently at a library. This man, whom I'll call Sam, had a talent for cutting diamonds, a feeling for form, a bright intellect and a good sense of humor. A year ago, I had brought him to a healing circle of friends. I was concerned for Sam because he abused alcohol and drugs and was wasting his talents. We in the group did not impose ourselves on Sam. We invited him to participate in our prayer group. We prayed over him, asking God to remove the negativity, the unproductive fear that stymies full expression. There was no apparent improvement in Sam. We left the results up to the Almighty.

Now it was a year later, and he could not wait to tell me this:

> I was feeling so low and down and out. Nothing was working in my life. As I lay on my bed in despair I cried, "GOD HELP ME!" Much to my surprise, I was suddenly and deeply aware of an energy force. It is hard to describe. It was like a bolt of lightning, the same energy that I felt in the healing circle a year ago, except then I was not ready. Now I was receptive. I felt a real peace come over me. I understood things differently. Look, I want you to know that I am back at diamond cutting. I, a Jew, went to some Egyptians I knew in the business, who were bitter competitors, and they helped me get started.

Guidance and Grace

Some 20 years ago, the controller for a large firm gave me a gift. It was a book written by Jiddu Krishnamurti. The title of the book I have long forgotten. The contents of the book were most provocative and spoke an ancient wisdom. Truth struck me to the core. What was being stated was not what we as a culture were practicing, and I decided it would be easier not to change my ways. Who wants to buck a well-established system of beliefs, both in oneself and in others?

Five years later something inside me was urging me to acknowledge Truth. I could no longer continue to suppress what I understood to be Truth. And so this book has been 15 years in the making for me. If this book stirs the Truth in you, so be it. I claim no ownership to Truth.

Another book stirred my soul even more, *Blessed Among Women*, by Arnold Michael. The Truth that Jiddu Krishnamurti was explaining in his book was being lived by the people in *Blessed Among Women*. Elizabeth, Anna, Mary, Joseph, Jesus and his cousin John lived Truth. The extended Holy Family is a wonderful example of guidance and grace, Law and Love.

The God-seed, the divine potential, is latent in everyone. Jesus and others have asked us to believe that. The people who know how to read the stars have said we have entered a new age, the Aquarian Age. Water is often used as a symbol for the Holy Spirit. In this new age, the dispensation of the Water Bearer is pouring forth the grace and guidance to enable us to *live* our divine potential. Belief is acceptance. *Performance is proof of our acceptance.* Jesus told us we could do greater things than he did. Jesus gave us a great example, and He never claimed to be a great exception.

The Two-Edged Sword

My friend and colleague Arnold Michael gives us this sage advice. He writes:

> Man is free to choose but he is not free from the *consequence* of his choices, not free from the law of karma or compensation or recompense. Without this choosing aspect of his divinity, man would be an automaton with a limited potential, such as the plants, insects, fish, animals, birds, etc. Man's potential, however, is a co-creator with the Father-Mother God; he is a God-seed and can only fulfill his divine destiny as a result of what he chooses to think, believe, feel, say, and do. If his freedom of choice were removed or restricted, his ability to become a God-like co-creator with his Source would be eliminated.

Michael further writes:

> Therefore, we could say that the nature of man's divinity is a *two-edged sword*: it is his greatest problem as well as his greatest asset. Why? Because the consequence of the way he uses his freedom of choice causes all his trouble, limitations and suffering, as well as all his attainments, achievements, abundance, happiness, peace, fulfillments

and joy. This is why *"Man, know thyself"* was over the door of the ancient hall of learning and why Solomon said, *"In all thy getting, get understanding."*

Guidance and grace cannot be separated. The law teaches us the consequence of our choices. Love empowers us to choose correctly. It is in our personal interest and the world's best interest to stay in tune with the Infinite. The God I believe in does not withhold grace, Love, law or consequence of choice.

Love is more profound than the avoidance of pain or the seeking of pleasure. "The Persian sage has said, *'Always meet petulance with gentleness, and perverseness with kindness. A gentle hand can lead even an elephant by a hair. Reply to thine enemy with gentleness. Opposition to peace is sin.'* The Buddhist says, *'If a man foolishly does me wrong I will return him the protection of my ungrudging Love. The more evil comes from him, the more good shall go from me.'* In the degree that we open ourselves to this divine inflow are we changed from mere men into God men" (from *In Tune with the Infinite*, by Ralph Waldo Trine).

My prayer is simple: "God, make me an instrument of Your will. I desire to express Love in all my thoughts, deeds and activities. Of myself I can do nothing; it is through You that I move and have my being. Thank You for providing all I require to express life fully."

Love's Pilgrim

Congratulations! If you have read this far, you have most likely chosen to be love's Pilgrim. You have chosen well to "be here" for God. Not for the God of superstition, dogma or creed, but as a representative of the most High. Not highfalutin', pompous or high-sounding, but expressing the higher vibration which includes all vibrations. Choosing to respond as an instrument of Love, choosing to give up reacting from fear, is Godlike.

Unenlightened Ways

We each move through phases of unenlightened ways of being in the world. The materialist, who is blind to real Love, mistakes lust for Love. The self-righteous are those who treasure self-importance, position and power. The sexually confused know carnal Love and fall short of expressing real Love. Another perversion of Love's power is living our life to please others, neglecting our own internal guidance. The pursuit and expression of real Love must be first. All else then is made available to us— peace, joy, blessed assurance and abundance. Love is premier. All else is promised to come to us. As long as we have a physical body, we will require food, clothing, shelter, transportation and each other. Within Love is all the intuitive intelligence we require. There is something in us that knows to live harmoniously and to provide for one another.

What Is Required of Us?

So what is required of us to express the real thing, Love Itself? To be a Love Pilgrim requires an awakening. It can be gradual or sudden. It can come out of suffering or enlightened understanding. It makes little or no difference if we are Buddhist, Christian, Confucian, Hindu, Jaina, Judaic, Islamic, Shintoist or Zoroastrian. What is important is that we awaken to Love. Nothing happens by accident. Our religion—or lack of one—is right for us.

Direct Revelation

Most religions are established through direct revelation of Truth. From the msytery of grace, divine truth reveals Itself through us. Love is impregnated within all of us. Hu is the (hue) light of God in *hu-man-kind*. God is Love, Light, Power and Truth. All inspiration comes from the Almighty. The direct impress of the Love waves is realized, and the particles light up in our auric field. Our thoughts are in alignment with the Father within. Our activities are aglow.

Love Is a Choice

Sometimes we are born into a religious family or we choose a particular religion because it is politically expedient. Sometimes in the name of religion we create war, destruction and devastation. That model is not acceptable to the awakened Love Pilgrim. The true religion within us knows Love is the answer. Love must be in the beginning, middle and end of all that we do, think and say. Deliberate choice is required to make love apparent in our lives.

We as Love Pilgrims awaken to the God-seed germinating within us; we begin to identify with what really is important. As we seek Its resemblance within us, the truth of our being is revealed. The beautiful essence of peace, Love, joy and assurance is obvious in our work, deeds and activities. "Faith without deeds is dead." St. James, Henry Drummond and other awakened beings know that Love is best expressed through the talents given us. Our talents expand with use and suffer with lack of use.

The Choice Is Ours

I can't—or maybe I can—tell you something about your potential talents. We each must seek out and act upon what we ourselves feel is right for us. M. Scott Peck, in *The Road Less Traveled*, writes this: "No words can be said, no teaching can be taught that will relieve spiritual travelers of the necessity of picking their own ways, working out with effort and anxiety of their own paths through the unique circumstances of their own lives toward the identification of their individual selves with God."

Being Here for God

Being here for God, knowing God as Love and serving God by expressing Love to one another is the task. Remember with me, love is forever expanding and never contracting; whereas fear contracts and reacts. The Love Pilgrim is loyal to understanding what Spirit is and honors It by expressing It. We Pilgrims claim ownership to Love, but not possessiveness.

"But owning this treasure brings its own responsibilities. Walking our own spiritual path means living according to the demands of our own truth. It means living a life that reflects our values, convictions, and goals accurately. It involves a continuous process of testing, questioning, and reevaluating our beliefs," according to Pythia S. Peay in the September 1992 issue of *New Woman* magazine. In the same article, called "Walking Your Own Spiritual Path," she expressed her feelings this way:

> I have often felt that those of us who walk our own spiritual path live on the frontier of the unknown: ready to face the unexpected turns and frightening obstacles of the strange terrain before us, guided only by our inner compass to an uncertain destination. But to step off our own path onto that of another, one perhaps more clearly marked than ours, is unthinkable; the road less traveled feels somehow right—and that's a good feeling.

Key to Empowerment

As each of us learns more and more to give ourselves over to Love, Love expands. "There are two sides to every vocation: unconditional giving of self to the call of God . . . and the gift of power which rewards the total gift of self to God," says Underhill. Remember, the silent partner is the Law. The Law returns to use with undaunted repetition what we put into it. Remember, also, that the Spirit of the Law is Love. Rechoosing Love is the way of the Love Pilgrim.

Yes, there are moments, sometimes too often, when we fall short of the mark. My wife might say, "Stop your whining, Chuck!" It is hard to break old habits but it is not impossible. It is difficult for me to see the good in criticism. Sometimes I feel criticism must be good because God knows I certainly do my share of it! There is a part of me that dislikes the gossiper or the critic—unless I am the one doing it. Now, if I really dislike someone for being critical, can I love myself the critic? No.

Gratitude Frees Us from Condemnation

"We must have a grateful feeling towards everybody and everything. . . . Love is the fulfilling of the Law . . . Only the heart that is above condemnation feels secure from condemnation . . . If anybody speaks to you critically, listen carefully. There is a ring of Divine Intelligence at your door.'' The quotes were taken from the lectures of a lady called the *teacher of teachers*. Her name was Emma Curtis Hopkins, a teacher and writer contemporary with Henry Drummond. In the late 19th and early 20th centuries she wrote and taught 12 classes in ''Scientific Christian Mental Practice'' and 12 in ''High Mysticism,'' both of which were later published.

How to Expand Love

How can we expand the Presence of Love in our life? Here are some suggestions: Invoke it. Affirm it. Surrender to it. Live it. Forgive ourselves and others for falling short of it. Express gratitude freely for the people and things that bring us pleasure, and let our gratitude spill over into the painful challenges of life that often become our greatest teachers. In our loneliness, let us remember God is Love. And as we learn to reside in Love, the Pilgrim is reconciled to the only-begotten One, begetting Love through Law.

Prayers

PRAYER OF INVOCATION: God, You are everywhere present. God, You are Love, and You are right here now.

PRAYER OF AFFIRMATION: God is Love. Love is making Itself known to me now, as me. I courageously express

my talents as my innermost desires, knowing I am guided
by Spirit and governed by Law. My actions are filled
with Love, and I am provided for in every way. I am a
beneficial presence unto the world. I am grateful for my
pilgrimage and the grace and the necessities of life to
fulfill it.

Thank You

I am most grateful for your interest in these writings and
thankful for all the solicited and unsolicited support and
criticism. I would like to leave you with several prayers.

A prayer of invocation was given to me by some
friends at Meditation Mount in Ojai, California. This
prayer is said daily in many languages, by many people
of different faiths. The second prayer is the prayer of St.
Francis of Assisi. St. Francis may not be the author; some
scholars now say that the author may be William the
Norman or William the Conqueror. Whoever is the author, thank you. By the way, there is an excellent movie
on the life of St. Francis that is available at video stores.
It is called, *Brother Sun, Sister Moon.*

The Great Invocation

From the point of Light within the Mind of God
Let Light stream forth into the minds of men.
Let Light descend on Earth.

From the point of Love within the Heart of God
Let Love stream forth into the hearts of men.
May Christ return to Earth.

From the center where the Will of God is known,
Let purpose guide the little will of men,
The purpose which the Masters know and serve.

From the center which we call the race of men
Let the Plan of Love and Light work out,
And may it seal the door where evil dwells.

Let Light and Love and Power restore the Plan
on Earth.

Prayer of St. Francis of Assisi

Lord [Divine Law], make me an instrument of Thy
peace; where there is hatred, let me sow Love; where
there is injury, pardon; where there is doubt, faith; where
there is despair, hope; where there is darkness, light; and
where there is sadness, joy.

O Divine Master [Presence], grant that I may not so
much seek to be consoled as to console; to be understood
as to understand; to be loved, as to love: For it is in giving that we receive, it is in pardoning that we are pardoned, and it is in dying that we are born to eternal life.

The next prayer was given me in New Zealand by a
medical doctor. He came as a guest to a seminar my wife
and I were teaching. Afterward he encouraged us to present more seminars, and he invited us to his humble

home, where Love's presence could be felt. His son informed us that his father was the first black man from India to graduate from medical school in New Zealand. The doctor used this prayer daily. It is called: "A Physician's Prayer"; the author is unknown.

A Physician's Prayer

Lord, Who on earth didst minister
    To those who helpless lay
In pain and weakness, hear me now,
    As unto Thee I pray.

Give to mine eyes the power to see
    The hidden source of ill,
Give to my hand the healing touch
    The throb of pain to still,

Grant that mine ears be swift to hear
    The cry of those in pain;
Give to my tongue the words that bring
    Comfort and strength again,

Fill Thou my heart with tenderness,
    My brain with wisdom true,
And when in weariness I sink,
    Strengthen Thou me anew,

So in Thy footsteps may I tread
    Strong in Thy strength always,

So may I do Thy blessed work
    And praise Thee day by day.

Perfect Love Casts Out Fear
(an Example of Affirmative Prayer)

God is perfect Love. God is all there is. God does not fear Itself. As I emerge out of the shadow of the Almighty into the Eternal, I know I am provided for in every way. The God-self within keeps me focused in the present moment. God, the all-Good, is right where I am. Fear is not part of God. I gladly release it to the nothingness from whence it came. Empowered by God, and moved by Love, I courageously accept life as it truly is. I confidently know I am guided. I humbly accept Your Will as my will, Your Power as my power, Your Life as my life. Thank you for showing me the Good in all. Amen.

Busy as a Bee in the Service of the Almighty

Love is the nectar we seek, It is gathered from each flower we meet.
As we buzz from here to there, Love's vibrations fill the air,
The pollen that we leave behind propagates more of the same kind.
We carry Love essence from where we roam to the center of our heavenly home.
The Queen of Heaven awaits us, to deliver Love's essence with acquiescence.
The essence forms a lovely home in the shape of a honey comb.
The Queen of Heaven gets off her throne to plant an egg in each cellular home.

The egg is protected in every way by the Mother of all, who is here to see the propagation of Love has continuity.
The drones that are born in this heavenly house serve the Almighty and Its spouse.
The heavenly nectar gathered by us is taken from all without a fuss.
The pollen we carry is doing its work, to bring forth the fruit of another day.
To some of us drones it seems like play to gather and deliver in this way.
We know our job and we do it well, we carry God-scent even to hell,
Our heavenly home resembles a dome where is found our honey comb.
The queen protects us in the dark of night, she helps us keep our heavenly site.
In the renewed vigor of the new day, the work goes on in a form of play.
Now you can see, we are busy as bees, propagating Love in the service of the Almighty.

Love Is Reality

Inwardly we seek that which we find has its origin in One mind.
It as a particle, It as a wave, expresses Life beyond the grave.
The only death is not to see the God within is in you and me.
Let's pray to know the self as One, Father, Mother, Christ as Son,

The triune God in everyone, is known to all, for all is One.

Christ as teacher is perfect Light, that restores us to our inward sight.

The master teaches us inner sight, the way to God is through Love and Light.

From the consequence of our choices, we are not free, unless we choose Love, as reality.

The law of karma is meant to be an instructive teacher, this we see.

Redemptive Love is the key that dispels the fear in you and me.

To know God as Love is a sacred trust; Its implementation is up to us.

O God, teach us this, we pray: to live Love dynamically in every way.

Charles Sommer

Bibliography

Aburdene, Patricia, with Naisbitt, John, *Megatrends for Women*. Village Books, division of Random House Inc., New York, N.Y., 1992.

Adams, Donald J., *Poems of Ralph Waldo Emerson*. Thomas Y. Crowell Company, New York, N.Y., 1965.

Bucke, Richard Maurice, M.D., *Cosmic Consciousness*. E. P. Dutton and Co. Inc., New York, N.Y., 1901.

Buscaglia, Leo F., Ph.D., *Born for Love*. SLACK, Inc., Thorofare, N.J., 1992.

Drummond, Henry, *The Greatest Thing in the World*. DeVorss & Company, Marina del Rey, Calif., 1994.

Holmes, Ernest, *The Anatomy of Healing Prayer*, Volume 2 of *The Holmes Papers* (Edited and collated by George P. Bendall, L.H.D.). DeVorss & Company, Marina del Rey, Calif., 1991.

Holmes, Ernest, *Ideas of Power*, Volume 3 of *The Holmes Papers* (Edited and collated by George P. Bendall, L.H.D.). DeVorss & Company, Marina del Rey, Calif., 1992.

Holmes, Ernest, *The Science of Mind*. G. P. Putnam's Sons, New York, N.Y., 1938.

Ostling, Richard N., "The Second Reformation." *Toronto Times.* Times Canada Ltd., Toronto, Canada, Nov. 23, 1992.

Peck, M. Scott, M.D., *The Road Less Traveled.* Simon & Schuster Inc., New York, N.Y., 1978.

Shahane, V. A., Ph.D., *Whitman's Leaves of Grass.* Cliff Notes Inc., Lincoln, Neb., 1972.

Trine, Ralph Waldo, *In Tune with the Infinite.* The Bobbs-Merrill Company, Inc., Indianapolis, Ind., 1970.

Underhill, Evelyn, *An Anthology of the Love of God* (Edited by Lumsden Barkway, D.D. and Lucy Menzies, D.D). Morehouse-Barlow Co., Inc., Wilton, Conn., 1976.

Recommended Reading

Fox, Emmet, *The Sermon on the Mount.* Harper & Brothers, New York, N.Y., 1938.

Hora, Thomas, *Existential Metapsychiatry.* PAGL Press, Orange, Calif., 1983.

Jampolski, Gerald G., M.D., *Love Is Letting Go of Fear.* Celestial Arts, Millbrae, Calif., 1979.

Siegel, Bernie S., M.D., *Love, Medicine & Miracles.* Harper & Row, New York, N.Y., 1988.

Sommer, Charles, *Licking Your Wounds.* DeVorss & Company, Marina del Rey, Calif., 1992.

AN INVITATION TO READERS

I am inviting you to participate in something special. Your level of spiritual awareness and skills is of real value. I am asking you to make a *small* written contribution to my new series of spiritual-awareness books. Please do so only if you feel motivated.

Also, if someone that you feel has a vital experience worth sharing, then please pass this request on to them as well.

The first book is about extraordinary events that happen to ordinary people, with emphasis on acute awareness to Divine guidance/assistance/help. Each contribution (story) to the book should be no more than one *typewritten* page. I would like the author's permission to edit and use the material. I reserve the right not to use the material. I prefer to use the contributor's real name and occupation in giving credit and acknowledgment. A substitute, fictitious name is acceptable. I will certainly respect privacy if that is wanted. Please, no drug-induced experiences. I want examples to be vivid, meaningful and real. Don't be concerned about writing skills; I just want the facts accurate. If you would like your material returned, please provide a self-addressed stamped envelope.

Your real-life examples are meaningful to me and others, especially when they come from your spiritual awareness.

I appreciate your interest. Send your material to:

CHARLES SOMMER
237 W. ALESSANDRO
SAN CLEMENTE, CA 92672-4334, U.S.A.